Contents

» RUNNING SAVED MY LIFE 1

» WHY I HAVE WRITTEN THIS BOOK AND INTRODUCTION. 3

» MY FIRST MARATHON – LONDON 1984 5

» SANTIAGO MARATHON, CHILE - ORA PRO NOBIS 9

» GOING THROUGH THE WALL – BERLIN 1990 13

» ATHENS MARATHON – DOG LEG ON THE OLD COURSE.
THE PATH TO ROME MARATHON 15

» RUNNING AND THE WEATHER - LESSONS ON RUNNING IN ALL WEATHERS 21

» THE BOSTON EXPERIENCE - 97TH AND 100TH MARATHONS - NO TEA PARTY FOR ME
PATRIOT GAMES– TERRORIST ATTACK 23

» FIVE MORE WONDERFUL LONDON MARATHONS
-1988, 1989, 1992, 1994 AND 1998 30

» DUBLIN'S FAIR CITY 1988 AND 1997 – CELT MEETS VIKING 36

» NEW YORK NEW YORK 1994 - SILVER ANNIVERSARY 39

» FOUR FAMOUS BELGIAN MARATHONS
– BRUSSELS, BERCHAM, ANTWERP AND BELGIAN COAST 43

» TURKISH DELIGHT, ISTANBUL 2003
EXPLOSIONS – ARMED GUARD AND BLACKOUTS 46

» MARATHONS FOR THE COMMITTED RUNNER 49

» BARCELONA TO LISBON MARATHONS
– CARRIED ON THE BACKS OF CATALONIAN PATRIOTS 53

» SCANDINAVIA: HELSINKI, STOCKHOLM, OSLO AND COPENHAGEN MARATHONS
-LAND OF THE VIKINGS AND MY WIFE AND NO MERMAID 56

» REYKJAVIK MARATHON 2004
- ICELANDIC SAGAS - COD WARS AND CELTIC MONKS 62

» CANADA – TORONTO 1999 AND NIAGRA FALLS MARATHONS - TEARS FOR 9/11 65

» RUNNING FOR THE CAUSES

» – THOMAS CORAM FOUNDATION LONDON - THE WORLD'S OLDEST INCORPORATED
CHARITY AND OTHER CHARITIES THAT I HAVE SUPPORTED 68

» VIVE LE FRANCE: PARIS IN THE SPRING 1988 – CHERBOURG 1994 (D-DAY 1944 50 YEARS
ON) AND REIMS MARATHON 1995 - THE CHAMPAGNE TRAIL 70

» WINTER MARATHONS FOR THE SERIOUS RUNNER 75

» EASTERN EUROPE: PRAGUE, BUDAPEST AND POZNAN MARATHONS -1968 INVASION – CHINA DOLLS – COPERNICUS AND CARMELITE MONKS. 78

» GOING DUTCH ROTTERDAM 1991 AND LEIDEN 2007 MARATHONS – SMALL BEERS AND ELECTRIC SPARKS 83

» ZURICH – SWISS AND NOT ON TIME 86

» FROM THE BALKANS TO THE BALTIC - SLOVENIA, LAND OF THE HORSEBURGER. LATVIA, UNDER ARREST 88

» EDINBURG 2005- THE MAN FROM HIBERNIAN AND TURBANS ON THE RUN 92

» MONACO MARATHON - GRAND PRIX AND 3 COUNTRIES IN ONE 94

» VIENNA – RUNNING FOR MOZART AND THE GIRLS OF ST PAUL'S SCHOOL, LONDON 95

» 1ST COLOGNE MARATHON 1997 AND MUNICH MARATHON 2007 – OCTOBERFEST BEGAN AT 40KM 97

» MILAN MARATHON - THE ICEMAN COMETH – SAN SIRO IN SPACE 99

» MALTA LAND ROVER 25TH MARATHON 2010 – GOING THE WRONG WAY HOME. 100

» NICE TO CANNES MARATHON 2009 – ALONG THE FRENCH RIVIERA 101

» BENIDORM MARATHON 2010 - ALONG THE SPANISH COAST. 102

» EPILOGUE - THE ROAD AHEAD 103

» MARATHON TIMES – 30 YEARS ON THE MARATHON ROAD , RUNNING IN 30 COUNTRIES 104

MARATHON ADVENTURES
ACROSS
EUROPE AND BEYOND

Thirty Years of Running Pain and Pleasure

Moses — Sláinte.
Keep an flag flying !
Seán Ó...

Sean A. O'Reilly

AuthorHouse™ UK Ltd.
1663 Liberty Drive
Bloomington, IN 47403 USA
www.authorhouse.co.uk
Phone: 0800.197.4150

Published by AuthorHouse 01/21/2014

ISBN: 978-1-4918-8669-4 (sc)
ISBN: 978-1-4918-8670-0 (e)

Library of Congress Control Number: 2013923074

authorHOUSE®

This Book is dedicated especially to all those Runners

who have raised Funds for Good Causes.

RUNNING SAVED MY LIFE

In 1988, I ran my first international marathon in Paris in aid of CORDA, a charity supporting research into coronary heart disease at The Royal Brompton Hospital in London. Little did I realise that in 2012 I would need the services of this hospital for a life saving double heart bypass.

In 2010 on our annual ski trip to Austria, I noticed that I was struggling to complete my usual after ski runs and put this down to getting on in age and running at high altitude. At Easter 2011, I completed the Milan marathon in 4-hours 23 minutes my slowest time ever. I put this down to the hot conditions—it was about 30 C at the finish. Some months later, I was struggling to keep running for three or more kilometres without having to walk, recover and then get going again. I had no problem completing moderate swimming sessions and bicycle tours of 2 or 3 hours. It was the extra energy required to run that was my problem. I realised that there had to be some sort of heart problem and instigated a series of heart tests. I had very good ECG and Echocardiogram results. A CTC scan showed a little above normal calcification of part of my coronary system. Finally, my consultant who was very interested in solving the problem performed an angiogram and even he was surprised with the result. He discovered a 99% blockage at the junction leading to two out of the three main coronary branches. He was amazed that I had no pain at rest never mind when I was running. He made the decision there and then to detain me in hospital. Five days later, I had my bypass at the Royal Brompton.

Some of my maternal uncles had died in their fifties from heart problems; but they were smokers and quite heavy drinkers. My father died at 88 years and my mother is still alive at 92 years old—although she has had a mitral valve heart problem for over twenty years. My siblings have had no heart problems so I was the one who drew the genetic short straw. If I had not noticed the deterioration in my running ability and had a more sedentary life style, my first heart attack would almost certainly have killed me.

I am pleased that I am running again and looking forward to my next marathon—in aid of CORDA.

"If you want to win something, run a 100m.
If you want to experience something then run a marathon."

EMIL ZATOPEK

WHY I HAVE WRITTEN THIS BOOK

Since my first marathon in 1984 there has been a revolution in the fitness industry. There are now Fitness Gyms in almost every town. Women and men can be seen running outdoors in all seasons across the globe. From half and full marathons we have moved on to biathlons, triathlons, ultra biking, running and swimming marathons and much else.

After thirty years of running for fun, fitness and various charities in over 30 countries, I am fortunate to have met some wonderful people and have had great adventures along the way. I have been surprised and humbled by the achievements of some extraordinary people. This book is an attempt to share my experiences and I hope it will inspire others to take up running for fun, fitness and adventure.

INTRODUCTION

The road ahead

For many people running is not for them. They believe they could never run a mile let alone the marathon distance of 26 miles 385 yards. Besides running can be boring and not a very social activity. Thankfully, the running boom of the 1980s made the armchair critics at least move forwards towards the edge of their armchairs. Events like the London marathon, completed by people of very different ages, shapes and sizes gave a new meaning and respectability to running. Today it is common to see male and female joggers plodding their way around our streets, lanes and byways and they can at times even outnumber the dog walkers.

My first encounter with running was more to do with necessity than with recreation or fitness. Life down on the farm as a young lad in Ireland often found me competing with our four legged friends who preferred the grass on the neighbouring farmer's side of the fence. Cattle unlike sheep do not respond to control by sheep dogs so it was down to me to round them up and save us from the wrath of our neighbouring farmers. My speed work was also enhanced by the daily three-mile track to school where to be late resulted in an encounter with a teacher's leather strap. Sometimes after milking the cows in the morning, I left too little time even for a brisk walk to school so I had to adopt the strategy of run, walk, run to get there on time. Little did I realise that I was doing fartlek training years before it became part of the runner's training programme.

Running as an end in itself, started for me at my secondary school in north London in the early 1960s. I can still remember our weekly school cross-country runs on London's Hampstead Heath. These normally took place in the early afternoon about 45 minutes after a good school dinner of suet pudding and over boiled cabbage followed by a large helping of steam pudding and custard from the generous dinner ladies. The whole lot was washed down by several bottles of free school milk that other pupils refused to drink—maybe because the milk was made from milk powder. Needless to state that my carbohydrate loading was maximised—I was ahead of my time with this idea—but I always found difficulty in converting my vast energy reserves into effective forward motion. For the afternoon run, scores of pupils from different schools were taken on free London County Council green buses to the Heath. We set off in a mass start and ran like bats out of hell straight up a steep hill. By the top, my first urge to be sick came over me. I was not the only one as faces turned green around me and then the pucking and retching began in earnest. After unloading some of my excess carbohydrates, I felt renewed and nearly always managed to finish in the top group of runners.

It was during the mid-sixties that I started jogging on the streets and parks of London for pleasure and fitness. I cannot remember seeing any other joggers on the streets in those days. There were no Nike trainers and designer wear to be seen anywhere. My running gear normally comprised an old pair of tennis shoes or plimsolls, football socks, shorts and tennis shirt—of the Fred Perry variety. If it was very hot I would wear a normal white vest. Luckily, I was young and thick skinned enough not to notice or worry about the strange looks I got from pedestrians and motorists.

Today and in my earlier days, I have always jogged to get fit to live the full life. This stems from a belief that to be fit in body helps to give one the potential to get mentally fit. I have never been the sort of person who lives to run, rather one who runs in order to be ready to participate in sports like golf, tennis, squash, cycling and in my earlier days football. However, the advent of the running boom in the 1970s did allow me to add a new dimension to my running sessions: the opportunity to participate in organised charity fun runs and marathons.

In 1979 I entered my first half-marathon and actually enjoyed the ordeal, mainly because I realised I was not the only person running with bowlegs and a receding hairline. It even seemed an alternative to pinting it down in my local pub on Sunday lunchtimes. In 1984, I took the final step up to the marathon itself and took part in the fourth running of the London marathon. This was a completely new experience for me, made memorable by the wonderful organisation and fantastic crowd support. Many of the runners wore fancy dress, as for me I managed to cover my receding hairline with two large stalks of pampas grass taken from my garden on the morning of the marathon. The trip from Greenwich to Westminster Bridge via the then desolate Isle of Dogs was no Lambeth walk for me. The excitement of the occasion and cheering onlookers got me as far as Trafalgar Square where I 'hit the wall'. I still managed to get down The Mall to finish on Westminster Bridge in 3 hours 9 minutes—my best ever marathon time. A few months later, I came back down to earth to run The Harlow Unigate Milk Marathon in Essex with a field of 900 odd runners, matched by the same number of spectators plus a few dogs. Amazingly, I enjoyed the experience in what I would now call a real runner's marathon—the bread and butter of the committed jogger. Alas, The Harlow Marathon is no more; but for me it was the start of my marathon adventures around the world.

"Though this be madness, yet there is method in it"

Hamlet, act 2, scene .2

M1 MY 1ST LONDON MARATHON 1984—
THE MARATHON STARTS HERE

3 AT FINISH OF MY FIRST LONDON MARATHON 1984 ACTUAL TIME 3HR 9MIN 10 SEC

'No Lambeth walk for me'

Saturday the 12th May was my father's 70th birthday and we organised a—special house and garden party for him with a traditional music band to add some atmosphere. It was the first and only birthday party that he ever celebrated. He had to be coaxed even to come, as he was never too keen to let people know his age. I think that working on building sites for many years with very fit younger men and most of whom thought that he was much younger than he really was gave him a certain amount of job security and kudos.

Sunday 13th May was marathon day when some 18000 runners would participate in the 4th running of the London marathon and I was one of the lucky ones to get selected to run. More than twice that number had failed in the lottery for entry selection. For once, I would be the most sober person at a party and would not, as was my usual habit, be one of the last to leave. For six months prior to the marathon, I had even given up my cigar habit and greatly reduced my alcohol intake.

Marathon training—I did it my way.

I like many other people at the time was swept away my marathon mania caused by the popularity of the first three London marathons, the film 'Chariots of Fire' and the publicised health benefits of jogging. A couple of runs in two local half marathons only helped to whet my appetite further for the full marathon experience.

I have always been active and at this time was playing local club football. I also played squash two or three times a week. In addition since my school days, I always tried to put in a couple of jogging sessions each week. I followed the mantra that you got fit to play squash and did not play squash to get fit. Nevertheless, a marathon demands a level of fitness, stamina and mental preparation that is above that required for most sporting activities. Careful reading of the running magazines indicated that I would have to devise my own training programme. The training schedules recommended by the 'experts' were very daunting in terms of the high weekly mileage recommended even for beginners. Most of schedules recommended only one rest day each week and little mention of any cross training – mind you there were very few Gym clubs around in 1984.

I joined my local athletics club and we did two evening runs a week of about eight miles which I found challenging. I did enjoy the company and learned quite a bit about pace and hill work but I did not like the idea of having to run at a fixed time of 6.30pm and then eat later. Some long distance runners tend to run alone in order to fit in family and work commitments.

For a sub 3hr 30min marathon the weekly mileage recommended could be as much as 50 miles with a long run of 18 miles+ on at least two occasions in the weeks prior to the marathon. Only once did I run a 50+ mile week, but my weekly average was about 25 miles with only one long run of 18 miles two to three weeks before the marathon itself. I did add a little variety to my runs to increase motivation and reduce boredom. Sometimes I did a session of just hill work, and a bit like the Duke of York, I led myself running up a hill and then led myself walking down the hill with a fixed rest period before repeating the exercise. However, I only did hill work when I felt reasonable fit. I also did farlek work around a 400m running track or around my local park which had a nice grass track where I live. I am very fortunate to be able to do about 80% of my runs on footpaths and grass tracks so avoiding tarmac roads and traffic fumes.

As I peaked in my training for my first marathon, I found that I got a bit more irritable and needed to sleep more, which with work and other commitments was not always possible. There and then I made up my mind that I would not run more than a maximum of 35 miles a week and I have stuck to this for the past 30 years. Yes, maybe I could have achieved a sub-3 hour marathon—even for my stocky muscular 80 kg+ frame – but that would have been too high a price to pay both physically and socially for me. Over the years, I have become a convert to cross training instead of pounding out the mileage. Sometimes I am surprised by the poor times achieved by some runners who put in high weekly mileage into their training. Recently I read a book on his running experiences by a Japanese novelist who ran consecutive monthly mileages of: 156,186,217 and 186 as he trained for the 2005 New York marathon. He failed to break 4 hours at 56 years of age and with a record of jogging for most of his life. At the professional end people like Paula Radcliffe, current women's world record holder, run up to 200miles a week. I like to think and rely on of the 5Ss of training: speed, strength, skill, stamina and spirit. It is no good having too much of one and too little of any of the others.

The London marathon was quite exceptional from its inception to the other big city marathons. Running for charity was a primary aim of many of the participants as well as the opportunity to provide a bit of fun by turning out in fancy dress. The English love to act and the London marathon was their stage, after all was not Shakespeare's Globe theatre near to the marathon course and as the great bard might have said 'If running be the food of love give me excess of it'

It came as no surprise when a charity got in touch and asked me to run for them. The charity supported aid for suffers of chronic and acute asthma. They invited me to participate in a photo shoot on Westminster Bridge in London and to do a jog over the bridge, which at that time was the finishing venue for the marathon. In the group with me were four other people: Alan Pascoe former Olympic hurdles medal winner, Jackie Genova – the Green goddess TV fitness guru and a police officer with his 14-year-old nephew who was a chronic asthma sufferer. Alan Pascoe also suffered from asthma and he told me at the time that he would love to run a marathon but could not because of his asthma. Whilst it was nice to get one's photograph in the newspapers there was the serious matter of raising some sponsorship money for the charity. Luckily as a teacher, I could tap the pockets of my fellow teachers and parents as well as relieving the children of some of their pocket money. I could also tap the resources of fellow football and squash members, my local pub and of course my relatives.

At that time, I did not rate 'asthma sufferers' as one of the neediest group of people for charitable support. It was only in 1997 when a close neighbour of mine, a lovely girl called Nadine died from a severe asthma attack. It was brought home to me what a life threatening illness it could be. I had a dance in the local pub with Nadine on her 21st birthday party. Little did I realise that two weeks later I would be at her funeral.

Since 1984, I have made a point of running for various charities, especially when running in big city marathons where there is a lot of competition to get a place. I would hate to think I took someone else's place in the knowledge that they might have raised a lot more sponsorship than me.

Preparation—The Oiling Up

For each of my six London marathons I got up around 6am and had breakfast of porridge and strong coffee. Then a shower to soften the skin of my feet, followed by giving them a good rub of calamine lotion and Vaseline in and around the toes. A careful application of Vaseline to other vital parts and a check on my running kit and I am off to the station for a 45 minute train and tube journey to Charing Cross, There I got on a very crowded train to Greenwich for the marathon start. After a last check on the local weather, I make my choice as to my running gear. A final rub down with Vaseline and I am ready for the 9.30am start. Sometimes I feel that I have already run a marathon before the official start.

In 1984 there was only one start for the marathon and we had no electronic timing chips to record our every move. I estimated it took me nearly 2 minutes to get to the starting line, which meant my photographed finishing time was 2 minutes over my real time. The marathon was held in mid May and it was a warm day with strong sunshine. Later London marathons now take place in April when cold and wet weather can be more of a problem. Unlike today, we had no balloon arches to mark the miles and no isotonic energy drinks or bananas. We were given plastic cups of water fished out of barrels—I hope the water did not came out of the Thames – every few miles but it tasted OK at least to those nearly dying of thirst.

The London marathon follows the tradition of the New York by staging the marathon course in several London boroughs. The first section of the course to Tower Bridge – a favourite spot for spectators – goes from Greenwich past the famous Cutty Sark ship at about 6 miles. There is always a large and supportive crowd for the London marathon. Many runners respond to this support by turning out in fancy dress. Even in 1984 we had scores of Elvis and Prince Charles characters. My contribution to the fancy dress party was to wear two large pampas grass stalks attached to my headband and acquired from my garden earlier on the morning of the race. Along the way, we were treated to music from several local bands not to mention London's Pearly Queens and Kings. As the pubs began to open, we were offered a free pint by the locals. Much later at the Munich marathon, I also had to turn down free jugs of lager offered by buxom German blonds. It is a real penance this marathon running at times.

There was one bleak part of the course in East London, which was a desolate demolition site of the former East London docklands. This area is now a new financial centre that includes Canary Wharf. At this stage of the race 17 to 19 miles, I was hitting the wall for the first time in my life. I was very pleased with my progress of a steady seven and quarter minute mile pace. London is not a good place to achieve a PB if one is running outside of 2hr 45 min pace. One tends to use a lot of nervous energy due to the sheer excitement of the occasion and the constant need to avoid and pass around other runners in a crowded field. At about 20 miles, I decided to run backwards for about 100 yards in order to ease the stress on some of my overused leg muscles. As I did so, I found that I could not run fast enough and as the runners approached, one lady from New York collided with me and we both fell down. Not a good idea and belated apologies to my long lost American cousin were in order.

As we approached the Tower of London, I felt Ok again and thought that I might even break 3 hours, but the stretch along the Thames Embankment was hard going in the ever-increasing hot sunny weather. At Trafalgar Square, I was struggling and stopped to try to drink some water This I managed despite my very shaky hands holding the plastic cup. The long run down the Mall and back along Bird Cage Walk to Westminster Bridge was a real struggle. The final stretch up the incline onto Westminster Bridge was a bit of a blur but I did keep going to finish in 3hr 9 min – which after 30 years of running marathons still remains a lifetime best.

After the race, I was greeting by my wife and two sons who managed to spot me on two occasions during the race. I treated them to a well-deserved ice cream and then it was the trek home and a long hot bath.

I was able to live off the buzz this marathon gave me for months afterwards. I managed to collect a decent some of money for the charity that I ran for and I still have their T—Shirt that I wore during the marathon.

"Suffering is the sole origin of consciousness "

Fydor Dostoevsky

40M SANTIAGO CHILE MARATHON APRIL 2005

Ora Pro Nobis

Santiago is a sprawling city of some 5 million souls. It is prone to smog due to pollution and to its location hemmed in between the high Andes and the sea. It has a chequered history in terms of democratic government and is afflicted by areas of severe deprivation. It is not a place that one would on first thoughts select for a marathon.

The main reason for going to Chile was to visit a cousin of mine, Sister Angela McKeever. Angela is a Catholic nun and has lived and worked amongst the poor of Santiago for over 30 years. In her own words, she has 'devoted my life to the people of Chile' and is very likely to end her days there. To me she is 'Mother Angela of Santiago' on a parallel with Mother Theresa of Calcutta.

Angela and I shared a similar childhood experience in Ireland. We both spent many years on farms away from our own families. Angela with her aged uncle and aunts and I with my maternal grandmother. We both worked hard on the farm taking on responsibilities way beyond our years. I specialized in milking cows and cattle grazing, Angela in supporting her uncle's greyhound racing enterprise, poultry keeping and gardening – not to mention housework. For me Gaelic Football was a passion and a great outlet for my excess energy and loneliness of living away from my family in London. Angela, apart from attending greyhound meetings, her interests took on a more spiritual dimension, often expressed by long hours of prayer in her local convent school and church. She came from a large family that produced priests, nuns and Christian Brothers aplenty. In those times in Ireland the only alternative to the church or farming or a few chosen professions was emigration. Her elderly aunts were keen for her to be part of the church because it would provide someone to pray for them in this world and in the next.

When I moved to England we lost contact but I did learn that she had become a nun and was in South America. Every few years she returned to Ireland via London and did manage to visit my mother on one or two occasions. As my marathon exploits developed, I made a mental note of getting out to South America to visit her and possibly run a marathon as well, I got her address and telephone number from my mother and was then at last after some 25 years I was able to make contact with her again. I was very impressed with the work that she was doing in Santiago, Chile. She lived amongst and worked with the poor of that city. She provided basic medicines, clothes and spiritual guidance to them. Many women had husbands in prison and she undertook to look after these families as well as visiting the prisoners themselves. In her area, families of 20 or more often lived in just two rooms. Children were out on the streets day and night and the winters can be cold and damp with dense smog. There was drug taking, police raids and sometimes shootings. In this at times mayhem, Angela strode at 5foot tall like a giant, fearless and totally respected by the poor inhabitants to whom she was their servant.

Of all the charities that I have supported over the years, the money that I raised for Angel's work was by far the most cost effective in terms of it use in going directly to providing basic medicines, food and clothing. There were no overheads like some of the big charities that often pocket more than 30% for themselves.

English is not widely spoken in South America. Prior to this trip I spent a year at evening class learning basic Spanish. I also took the opportunity to look up some of the troubled history of South America.

My first inkling that this was going to be a very different experience to my other marathon runs came with registration problems. I paid my registration in US dollars, which was sent by secure named recorded delivery. The name used was the chief organiser of the marathon and I made sure to email him. After some weeks I had heard nothing so I emailed him and he replied that he had received nothing from me. I emailed again to the effect that he had signed for the delivery—this I was able to check separately. Some time later, I resorted to Sister Angel's help and then he claimed that he had only received 'some' of the money – someone else had taken the rest. However—and very generous of him—he would allow me to enter the marathon. When I registered for the marathon in Santiago I made sure that he met Sister Angel in person. He was a little red faced to say the least. I can only hope he had a lesson on the evils of stealing.

Getting to Santiago proved to be more difficult than I had anticipated. A delayed flight with Iberian Airlines to Madrid meant that I missed my connection to Chile. After some hours at a deserted Madrid airport I talked my way onto a 3am flight to Montevideo in Uruguay – at least it was in South America. We arrived in the middle of a thunderstorm and on getting out of the aircraft in pouring rain, we were greeted with flashes of lightning and tremendous bangs of sound along the perimeter of the airport. Welcome to the next revolution I thought. After more hours of waiting I got an Argentina Airways plane to Santiago. My dear cousin Sister Angela was there waiting for me. I was her first relative to visit her in South America in over 30 years.

There are two striking things that one notices on first visiting Santiago: wild dogs and buses. The buses are nearly always full. There are hundreds of them and belch out thick black diesel fumes not to mention noise. They form almost a continuous line along the main Avenue Bernado O'Higgins, which is several kilometres long and was part of the route for the marathon course. There are plans to introduce bigger more efficient buses, but at present their fumes and noise pervades the whole city.

There are even more dogs than buses—at least to me it appeared that way. Like the buses, they too would be fellow participants in the marathon. I hope, like me, they did not have to register. Despite being wild, the dogs were very friendly and well liked by the inhabitants. They are all interbred to have a uniform size and colouring. On one occasion, I saw a dog and bitch stuck back to back after a love making sessions. Dogs, unlike humans, cannot just roll over after love making. Both dogs looked very sorrowful and forlorn to the amusement of the watching children and adults. On another occasion I saw a bitch sitting very firmly on the ground so as to discourage any amorous attention from other dogs.

Santiago in April can still be hot and humid. I began to worry about the wisdom of running a marathon in this city and noticed that maybe I was not the only one as most of the runners had only entered for the half marathon. My confidence was restored when I realised that I had one of God's representatives on earth supporting me—namely Sister Angela. When I saw how she lived and worked with the poor, travelled on those crowded buses in torrid summers and freezing winters, I realised that her hard working days on the farm in Ireland had in someway prepared her to survive in this city. I had come along way and was not going to let her down now.

On the Sunday morning of the marathon, I headed for the start and Sister Angel headed for the church. The starting area was a pleasant enough park—with plenty of dogs of course. There was time to mentally prepare for the task ahead. At 9am, we were on our way. Soon we were out on the main Avenue Bernado O'Higgins. At this point the buses and dogs joined in big time. It was already getting hot and smoggy. The buses had two-thirds of the avenue and the dogs and runners the other one third. The buses went up and down the road showing their support by belching out plumes of black smoke and the occupants of the crowded buses were frantically waving and shouting at us. Did they really want us to join them on the bus?

I began to have second thoughts. Could this be the first marathon that I would not complete? Then I remembered that Sister Angela was praying for me in the church and a spiritual wellbeing came over me. It was a long slow uphill incline for several kilometres towards the invisible Andes in the distance. I now had reached the point of no return and my survival was clearly not entirely in my own hands. I was reliant on spiritual nourishment as well as physical. The dogs and buses became fewer in number and I began to feel at last that I was in a marathon—even more so when most of the runners peeled away towards the half—marathon finish.

My training for this marathon as usual broke most of the guidelines for marathon running—mostly I do much too little. I nearly always spend February half-term skiing in Austria and the Easter holiday skiing in Norway – my wife's country. Some of my runs are on snow and it can be very cold but at least the air is fresh. As this marathon was in mid–April, I did not have too much time to run in England before leaving for South America. I still am fortunate to be able to keep a reservoir of fitness and stamina to call on as I train all year round.

After about 15km I met up with a Canadian in his mid-thirties who I noticed was carrying his wallet and passport in his left hand. I got talking to him and he told me that he was staying in a Youth Hostel and did not want to take the risk of leaving his valuables at the Hostel. He had previously run a marathon in Nairobi in Kenya and deployed a similar technique there. In my book to run 42 km holding a largish wallet in your hand is an achievement in itself.

He was hoping to get round in under 4 hours, a similar target to mine, and as there were so few marathon runners it seemed a good idea to run together. After 30km, we turned for home to head down Avenue Bernado O'Higgins and rejoin our fellow dogs and buses. By now, the traffic had increased and there was a police officer and another man with a red flag at each intersection. The real fun was about to begin.

As we approached an intersection it looked as though nothing was going to stop those determined Chilean drivers. We were getting tired by now and one had to concentrate on just keeping running. Often we were only meters away from the cars when they were finally brought to a stop by frantic waving of the red flag and the raising of the police officer's baton and the simultaneous blowing on his traffic whistle, As we crossed, we were greeted by a crescendo of hooting car horns. At first, I thought that this was a Chilean motorist way of supporting the runners. On second thoughts, I was not so sure as I experienced a similar control system in the last 10km of the Athens marathon. Then I knew for sure that the Athenian motorists do not like obstacles of any description in their way.

Towards the finish, we passed the Chilean National Football Stadium. This stadium was used for purposes other than football and pop concerts under the Augusto Pinochet regime in the 1980s. Under his military dictatorship, thousands of people were held in the stadium before finally disappearing. Similar methods were used in neighbouring Argentina around the same period.

My Canadian partner stayed with me until the last 2km when I slowly pulled away from him but by then I knew he would achieve his target of under 4 hours. I finished in a time of 3hr 49 min—a miracle given the circumstances. Clearly Sister Angela's prayerful intervention had worked.

I sometimes try to get a second medal from the finishing marshals if someone has been supportive of my efforts. I am pleased to state that Sister Angela's Santiago marathon medal is proudly on display next to a crucifix in her lounge. For Sister Angela life is a spiritual marathon and when she crosses the finishing line at the gates to heaven, I am sure that race marshal St Peter will present her with her heavenly medal.

The next day we were able to visit some of the homes of people where Sister Angela lives and performs her earthly tasks.

Despite their obvious poverty, I was impressed by the dignity and pride of many of the people I met. One particular family that I met was headed by a Mapuche Indian lady who was married to a local man from Santiago of Spanish descent. She was proud of her many children and of her Indian origin. Sister Angela translated her answer to my questions about the Mapuche Indians.

For centuries the Mapuche owned most of the lands in south Chile. The Spanish Conquistadors set about taking these lands much as their north European counterparts in North America. The Mapuche were partially successful in their resistance and there are still one million Mapuche out of a total population of fifteen million Chileans. Part of the conquered lands contains a monoculture of extensive forests that gives little work to the Mapuche. The wood is exported to the US and Europe yielding great profits for the local big landowners. In the 1880s, after further violent military expeditions, the Mapuche Nation was incorporated into the state of Chile. A lot of Mapuche were transferred to reservations to live in abject poverty. Recently anti-terrorist laws were used by the dictator Augusto Pinochet to suppress Mapuche rebellions. Sadly under the current more democratic set up the laws are still employed to continue to deprive the Mapuche of their lands and living. The Mapuche lady of the house showed me her Indian headdress and some photographs of her in full Mapuche dress when she lived in her homeland. I even got a chance to play the Mapuche drums. All I can say is what I said in that house. Viva La Mapuche. A week later I visited Argentina on my way home and noticed that there were few native Indians left in that country.

Part of the title for this section included 'Ora pro Nobis' which means pray for us. Thank you Sister Angela for all those prayers and may you continue with the wonderful work that you are doing for the poor of Chile.

"To conquer one self is a greater task than conquering others"

Gautama Buddha

M8 BERLIN MARATHON 1990

Backs to the Wall

Of all my marathons, this one had the most emotional start and was historically for me on a par with the running of the 100th Boston marathon. Berlin on several occasions has been the fault line between freedom and oppression. One recalls: the Hitler Berlin Olympics and the marching Nazi columns through its streets; the famous photograph of a Soviet soldier placing the Red Flag of Communism on the roof of the burnt out German Reichstag building; the memorable speech of President Kennedy in West Berlin next to the wall saying 'Ich bin ein Berliner' and the visit of Barack Obama in 2008 speaking for a free world where people of all races can live and work.

In 1989, the first cracks began to appear in the wall that divided Berlin. The wall formed part of what Churchill termed the 'Iron Curtain' that stretched from the Baltic to the Balkans. It was the front line in the cold war between two ideologies: collective communism and individual capitalism. Unfortunately Soviet style communism was a big departure from the communism envisaged by Karl Marx and it had to depend on totalitarianism and control of the individual's rights of free speech and movement.

Soon the cracks became gaps allowing the free movement between East and West Berlin. The cold war was over. Prior to 1990, the marathon only took place in West Berlin with the symbolic start at the wall itself – literally, the runners had their backs to the wall. This time it would be very different. Now the start was about a mile from the wall and we would run towards the Brandenburg Gate and into East Berlin. In the words of Hugh Jones the 1982 London marathon winner and pacemaker for this race: 'We came from all corners of the world, 25,000 runners from 60 countries competing in the first all Berlin marathon since the 1936 Olympic marathon in the city . . . . We received a tumultuous reception from spectators as we emerged into East Berlin from the Brandenburg Gate. Five miles later, we were making an uncomfortable return to the west. The remnants of the wall were under our feet, hostility hastily buried under a patchy layer of tarmac.' The front pages of the world's press captured the historic moment as the runners ran through the Brandenburg Gate. I vividly remember a bank of hundreds of photographers waiting in the middle of the wide road for our entry. I recall the tall soviet built TV tower that had acted as a big brother symbol to keep Eastern Europe in check. Along the bleak open streets of East Berlin there was sullenness in some of the local residents and East German guards. It was still 3 days before official reunification on the 3rd October and I have a lasting impression of the drab prefab concrete flats and the odd fibreglass Trabant cars parked along the streets. The early yellow-brown autumn leaves were swirling in the breeze around the pavements and there was a strange grey eerie emptiness, which in turn induced a silence in all the runners. It was as if this autumn decay was symbolising the end of the old communist regime and its cruel absolute power over the people.

Back through no man's land and towards the west our spirits began to lift and as the number of spectators increased it began to feel that we were at last running a big city marathon. As we ran the long trek past the Zoological gardens towards Kursfmam, the commercial centre of West Berlin, I recognised the streets that my wife and I had to walk alone in the early hours of the morning of the previous day.

My wife as a teacher of German wanted to experience East Berlin before things became too westernized. On the Friday morning, we took a train to Alexanderplatz in the heart of old Berlin. As we walked along the famous Unter den Lindern towards the Opera House, I was reminded of the decadent Berlin of the 1930s as depicted in the film Der Blaue Engel and starring Marlene Dietrich. At the Opera House, we were able to book box office tickets for the evening performance of La Traviata for only £5 a seat. Whilst trying to book the tickets I was ignored by the two women in the booking office whose morning chat was more important than attending to customers. I did let them know in German that they would be in for a bit of a shock when capitalism took hold in the east. I think that they must have been intoxicated by their newfound wealth when the Ost mark was converted overnight to the same value as the Deutsh Mark. Like their fellow East Germans they would soon come to realise that capitalism can have no gain without pain. Later we went to a nearby café and met some older East Germans. Some of them had a pre war naval background and we were astonished to find that they were expressing Old Prussian Teutonic values of superiority and it was as if communism never happened. After this surprise we decided to get a train and go a few kilometres deeper into East Berlin to hopefully meet some 'real' East Berliners. A few stops along the line we saw some very large complex of beehive shaped blocks of flats and decided to visit them. As we drew near we noticed that there was a café in the basement of one of the blocks and decided to go in and order a coupe of beers. One customer on hearing us speak English rushed over, introduced himself as a lecturer from the local further education college, and said that we were the first people that he had met from the West. To celebrate the special occasion he insisted that we share a bottle of fine Crimean champagne with him and as my wife speaks very good German, it was not long before this man revealed his life story. In doing so we drank two more bottles of Champagne but at least we got to pay for one of them. He told us that he lectured in motor mechanics and he realised that Trabant two stroke engine cars would not be quiet able to compete with Porsche and Mercedes technology, so the future work wise for him was bleak but he looked forward to the new freedom and the opportunity for travel and retraining in the West.

Needless to state we arrived well inebriated and late for the opera, and duly stumbled into our box seats. I cannot image what such seats would have cost at Covent Garden in London. After the opera we decided to sober up a bit and visit a café where we got in more conversation and at midnight we left to get a train to take us back the 5kilometers or so to West Berlin. To our surprise we found the station was closed and there was only one option for us – a long walk back through no man's land to the West. We walked past the empty Reichstag and through the Brandenburg gate. There were few people and no cars around and soon we were completely alone and isolated between East and West Berlin It was extraordinary to contemplate that we would be one of the last people to experience the desolation of landscape and suppression of free speech and movement that represented the cold war. In just over 24 hours, 25,000 runners would be running on the very road that we were now standing on and soon after that there would be traffic and human movement on this main reopened road night and day in the future. We got to our hotel around 3.30am and Saturday was definitely going to be a day of rest.

As for the marathon itself, I was fully rested by Sunday morning. The weather was cool, cloudy and dry, ideal condition for running. I was able to finish the race in 3hr 28 min as expected. Afterwards my wife and I enjoyed our first Japanese meal served in traditional surroundings and style; but before that of course I managed a couple of Guinness in an Irish Pub.

Our flight home was delayed by two hours and we arrived in London when the tubes and trains were closed so it was a taxi ride to my parent's flat in North London. My wife and I got up very early on Monday morning to join the mad rush to get to our respective schools and soon our trip to Berlin was just a distant memory; but one that will stay with us for the rest of our days.

"If you feel bad at 10 miles you are in trouble. If you feel bad at 20 miles, you are normal. If you do not feel bad at 26 miles you are abnormal"

Rob de Castello

FROM ATHENS TO ROME

7 M THE ATHENS MARATHON 1989

Running the old course, the dog leg.

The Greeks had no race in the ancient Olympic longer than about 3 miles. They raced in a stadium barefoot between poles and runners could push, pull, trip and kick sand in the face of their opponents as they ran around the poles. The Greeks did employ inter—city messengers who ran long distances, but they were not athletic heroes; they were the elite mail carriers of their era. Pheidippides was such a runner.

Myth has it that Pheidippides in 490 BC ran the 25 hilly miles from the scene of the battle of Marathon to Athens to announce the victory over the Persians. He is reputed to have said 'Rejoice. We conquer' and then dropped dead. The Athenian army outnumbered by 6 to 1 had killed 6500 Persians in their victory at

Marathon. Herodatus recorded some facts on the battle but no dying scene. He did write about a Pheidippides who ran 150 miles in 48 hours to Sparta to recruit help prior to the battle.

Plutard, 50 years later, wrote of a runner messenger named Eucles who ran to Athens and then dropped dead and before doing so proclaimed 'Rejoice we conquer'.

Time compresses and edits history to generate an essential myth.

In the 19th century, students were taught the heroic compressed story of Pheidippes's sacrifice. The idea of the supreme sacrifice tied nicely in with the rise of nationalism and patriotism.

ATHENS OLD OLYMPIC STADIUM WITH DAUGHTER

The ancient Greek Games were revived by the Frenchman Baron de Coubertin and the first modern Olympic Games were held in Athens in 1896.The marathon run was included and was from the village of Marathon, scene of the ancient battle, to the newly built marble clad Olympic Stadium near the Acropolis in central Athens. The marathon distance was 25miles (40 kilometres) and appropriately won by a Greek. This same course—but 2.2km longer—and stadium was the venue for the last Olympics in Athens in 2004. To get the extra distance a detour round the tomb of the Unknown Soldier celebrating the battle of Marathon was included in the course.

As one of the many thousands of runners who failed to get a place in the 1989 London Marathon, I was pleased to discover that it was possible to get a place in the October running of the Athens Marathon. Like other big city marathons, Athens had only recently set up its own marathon based on a similar course to the one used in the 1896 Olympics. I was surprised that there were only about 2000 entrants for such a historic marathon course.

The weather for the marathon was fine with an average temperature of 22 C which was a little on the hot side. The course was similar to a dog leg on a golf course with a long straight stretch going south down the coastal road, then swinging inland south westwards up a long climb from 17 to 20 miles and then downwards towards the Acropolis and the old Olympic stadium. I found the first half of the marathon very enjoyable with the run round the monument of the Unknown Soldier surrounded by a small olive grove very moving. We were joined by the odd dog now and again, but sadly as we got closer to Athens one could not help but notice the number of dead dogs and cats along the road side. The climb at 17 miles was one of the toughest I have ever encountered. The increasing temperature and direct heat from the sun made the climb more difficult. Heartbreak Hill on the Boston marathon is modelled on Athens but is a gentle incline compared to its Athens equivalent. I made it non—stop up the long hill; but nothing prepared me for the last 6 miles down to the stadium.

By now the Athenians were out of bed and doing what they do best – driving their cars at speed and using their car horns as the main method of steering and breaking or should I say non-breaking. Every 500 meters or so there was a junction with a police officer and a man with a big red flag. By this stage in the race the runners were well spaced out so often one approached a junction alone and hoped the traffic would be stopped by the policeman waving frantically his white gloved hands and the man jumping up and down waving his red flag. One's life really was in the hands of the Greek Gods. The cars would scream to a stop and the crescendo of horn blowing would reach a continuous cacophony. Did the frantic distorted faces of the drivers pressed up against the windscreen signal their joy at seeing a marathon runner in the home of marathon running? After a few episodes of this reception, I quickly concluded that Athenians hate any obstacle: human, dog, cat or anything else getting in the way of their car. Nike may be the goddess for runners representing victory, speed and strength: but the goddess for Athenian motorist has to be Mania representing 'insanity'. Nike is one of the Greek Gods with wings; maybe we could have called on her support for those last 6 miles of almost hell on earth. Some years later, I was to have a similar experience on Avenue Bernado O'Higgins in Santiago, Chile.

As the view of the Acropolis grew clearer, bigger and nearing with the lovely marble clad Olympic stadium nestled below the hill, my spirits lifted and now there was a chance that I would reach the stadium and not end up like those unfortunate dogs and cats along the way. As I entered the stadium it was wonderful to see the smiling faces of my wife and three year old daughter, Astrid. A sprint down the home straight gave me a time of 3hr 25min. – in line with my expectations at that time.

The Olympics would return to Athens in 2004 and the same marbled clad stadium would be used for the finish of both the women's and men's marathons. At that time the UK had a world marathon record holder, namely Paula Radcliffe. She was the favourite to win the gold medal but the very hot weather and the tough course got the better of her. She failed to finish and ended up sitting on the kerbside in tears. This is not a world record-breaking course and neither was it for Pheidippides 2500 years earlier! There is a big difference between running a city marathon and an Olympic marathon. The strategy for the later is not about a good time but about beating your fellow competitors who are going to give it everything. For many of them it is going to be there only chance of competing in an Olympic event. I am reminded here of the great Ron Clarke who broke the world record several times at 5km and 10 km; but never won an Olympic medal after several attempts.

After the race, my daughter ran her first 50m on the Olympic track crossing the finishing line in some style. In the years to come she would run with me on some of the half-marathon parts of marathon courses. This was also the first time my wife and I visited the Mediterranean area and so the week after the marathon was an opportunity to visit some of the Greek islands and the sights of Athens. The week is particularly memorable for one incident.

Whilst walking along the beech near marathon I noticed some wild dogs around. I was not sure if rabies was endemic in Greece; but because of strict quarantine regulations, Britain and Ireland are free of this terrible disease. As we passed a large house with wrought iron closed gates, I stood close to the gates to get a good view of the house and its splendid surrounds when a guard dog appeared and put his head through the space between the bars in the gate. He bit me on the thigh and drew some blood. My first thought was that the dog might be a rabies carrier so it was straight to the local doctor. I was worried until the doctor told me that rabies was not present in the area. All guard dogs are vaccinated against the disease. What a relief. After a good dousing with Iodine I left the surgery a very relieved man.

The old marathon course with its dogleg shape had certainly tested my running ability and a local dog had left his mark on my leg as a souvenir.

The Path to Rome

In my teens I was introduced by my brother-in-law to a book titled 'The Path to Rome' written in the 19C by Hilaire Belloc. His walk was a spiritual Odessy to Rome. He took every opportunity to engage with local people as he walked through eastern France, Germany, over the Alps and along the Apennines down into Rome. He made his walk that bit more challenging by trying to make his path the shortest and most direct route to Rome as well as trying to attend Mass every day.

I was attracted by a walk or even a bike ride to Rome rather than just flying there and savoring the idea of a bit of an adventure with the spiritual dimension being a possible bonus.

My journey to Rome happened when least expected and the path was a very different route to the one taken by Belloc.

As mentioned elsewhere in this book, we have some very close German friends that we first met in Germany in 1977. The very first Germans that we befriended were a lovely young German couple, with a beautiful baby girl called Christina. They had finished their studies at Bonn University and helped us to acquire their student flat to accommodate my wife and two sons for their year long stay while by wife studied at the University. Some years later a very attractive blond 16-year-old German girl – namely Christina – stayed with us as part of a six-month placement in the sixth from of a local school. A few years later her mother and father visited us as part of a tour round England. Her father Ludwin had arranged some short stay exchanges between students at his college and my own school in Berkhamstead. On one such visit just before Easter 1996 Ludwin, whilst staying with us, offered the use of a caravan that he was going to take to a beautiful campsite at Anguillara along Lake Braccino just 16 miles north of Rome. This offer was by way of a thank you for the school partnership exchanges and for having his daughter in our home.

Rome! The memory of Belloc's 'Path to Rome' book came flooding back to me. I told Ludwin that I had always wanted to go to Rome but it had never been by intention to fly or drive there. Still I was not going to turn down the offer of free accommodation on a campsite just a short bus ride from the eternal city. A couple of weeks later I went to Boston to participate in the 100th running of the marathon. When I returned from Boston I picked up a letter in my hallway with unusual black lines around the edge of the envelope and a German postmark. I opened it and I was shocked to read in German that Ludwin had died age 46 years old. He had been born with a slight congenital heart defect and during the Easter vacation had felt unwell and was taken to hospital where he died within 24 hours of admission, probably due to a viral infection of the heart valve.

Some weeks passed until I spoke to his very distressed wife Hannelore – their's had been a marriage made in heaven—and she suggested that we could take the caravan which had been recently purchased in Germany to Rome as the very popular campsite had already been booked. It was decided that we would come to their home town of Aachen to collect the caravan and take Hannelore's youngest children aged 11 and 13 with us to Rome. Hannelore would fly out later to join us. The call to Rome had come sooner than expected and my path would be from London to Bonn and then towing a caravan through Germany, Switzerland and northern Italy.

It seemed strange to spend one's summer holiday with a grieving family. It was very difficult to know how to relieve the constant pain of grief, particularly for Hannelore. We went to some open-air concerts and on occasion, I walked along the lakeside with her. Although the area brought back memories for Hannelore of the lovely summers spent here with her husband and family, it was also comforting for her to be in a place where she shared so many happy moments with Ludwin. There was a particular high point of this trip, which occurred when we visited St Peter's. On Hannelore's advice we took the early bus into Rome and were first in the queue to get into the Sistine Chapel. Hannah told me to go ahead and follow the signs – quite a long way—to get to the Chapel and I arrived in the Chapel five minutes before anyone else. I lay down on the floor and spent several minutes looking up at Michelangelo's famous Sistine Ceiling in spiritual bliss. The outstretched finger of the hand of God just touching the upwards stretching index finger on the hand of Adam offering him the gift of life was very moving .Later it occurred to me that this image reflected the now heavenly and spiritual love between Hannah and Ludwin. We walked up the Cupola to get a magnificent view of the hills of Rome and of Ancient Rome. I looked northwards towards Britain and Ireland, and thought of Belloc walking all that way on his own over a hundred years ago.

In 1996, our daughter Astrid was 10 years old. She had made friends with an older Italian girl called Julia from Rome at the campsite. Three years later Astrid and I would be back in the Eternal City not only to meet Julia but for Astrid to do her first competitive 5km run and for me to run the Rome Marathon. This time we would be going by plane as we only had the weekend off before being back in school on Monday morning.

We got to Rome late on Saturday evening and after avoiding some dodgy taxi drivers eventually got an ' official city ' taxi—even then the driver still managed to overcharge us – to our hotel ' The Pyramids. An unusual name for a hotel in Rome, but the city did owe a lot to the cultures of Egypt and Greece. It was fortunate that Julia's father had already picked up our race numbers as we were late for registration.

We were up early on Sunday morning and were pleased to meet Julia in the hotel lobby as she smoked her second cigarette of the day. We walked to the Coliseum and it was not long before Astrid and I were off on our 5km and 42km runs respectively. Both races started and finished at the Coliseum. After Astrid finished her race Julia took her sightseeing and for lunch in her apartment near the Vatican.

The weather was very pleasant with a starting temperature of about 18 Celsius and sunny. It did get a little warmer as the morning progressed so a very good marathon time was not on the menu for me. The course was essentially a single lap taking in most of the great sights of new and ancient Rome. We started in front of the Coliseum, down the Via Cavour, past the ancient Forum to the Piazza del Papollo and across the Tiber to St Peter's Square. Then along the Tiber past the 1972 Olympic Stadium along the Via del Foro Italico to again cross the Tiber and come back to Villa Ada, past the Stadio Flaminia and back to the Piazza del Popolo. Then to the Spanish Steps, the Trevi Fountain – no time to throw any coins into the fountain – past the famous Pantheon, around the Coliseum towards the Circus Maximus. On to the English Graveyard – burial place of the English poet Byron, past the Pyramids (close to our hotel of the same name) to San Paulo and then back up again past the Ancient Baths to finish next to the Coliseum. The course was a journey through Rome down the centuries taking in most of the key attractions. It was the most cultural and historical route of all the marathons that I have run so far.

Memorable moments include: the enthusiastic clapping of the runners as we ran through the narrow Via Del Corso, which returned the compliment by echoing back with several reverberations. At the Piazza Navona, with the Pantheon in front of us, we got so close to the waiters—who were weaving their way through the runners to serve the outdoor customers – that, I had to resist the temptation of taking a quick espresso off one of their trays. It would have cost less as you pay more for a coffee in Rome if you take it sitting down. I got to half way in 1hr 51min; a little slow for me but enjoying the scenic run was much more important than trying to beat my personal clock. As the temperature rose, I began to struggle a bit more and was glad that I had decided to run in shorts and thin running vest. I can always measure my heat output by how many times I have to wring the sweat out of my headband and by the end, it was getting to be about every 3 minutes. It was strange that I should be passing the Circus Maximus and then the longish run to the Coliseum when I was suffering the most as these two places in ancient times saw great suffering and even death from the competitions that they engaged in to satisfy the more sadistic needs of the Roman citizens and their Emperors.

I finished in 3hr 47 min but the whole experience of this run was the abiding memory for me. My daughter Astrid had a very good 5km run and felt that she could have run much faster which is always a good feeling and hope for the next run. After a rest in my hotel, Astrid and Julia came back and we went out for a bit more site seeing, this time with a born and bred Roman. We went to an Italian style restaurant and a very good violinist serenaded my daughter. Soon it was arrivederci to Julia and time for the flight back to London and school for both of us on Monday morning.

Later in the week the local paper had a headline 'End of the Road for School's Marathon Man'. I was due to end my career as a full-time teacher in senior management and take up new opportunities in the private sector. In my 11 years at this school, I had started with the Athens marathon and finished with the Rome marathon going from one ancient city to another. More marathon adventures lay ahead.

My path to Rome had taken many unexpected twists and turns. The memories will stay with me for life.

RUNNING AND THE WEATHER

READY FOR TRAINING RUN IN NORWAY

In February 2009, London came to a standstill by some 15 cm of snow overnight with all bus and most tube services suspended. As my wife's school in London was closed, we decided to get the skis out and go on a 15km cross-country trip in good skiing conditions. Work and school was suspended for many adults and children, who then took the opportunity to come out to enjoy the snow using a variety of improvised toboggans. Children even put their computers and associated facebook and you-tube on hold to throw snowballs and make snowmen. No doubt, they returned to their computers later in the day to post their experiences.

What was described as the heaviest snowfall for twenty years had the effect of getting more people outdoors than even on a glorious sunny day during the school holidays. In my view, this supports what John Ruskin said about weather:

*'Sunshine is delicious, rain is refreshing, wind braces us up,
snow is exhilatering: there is really no such thing as bad weather,
only different kinds of good weather.'*

I add to this the old adage that there is no such thing as bad weather only wrong clothing and I have always enjoyed running within reason whatever the weather conditions. The idea of getting out of the house and experiencing nature and the weather is uplifting. I am happy to walk, run, bike or participate in ball games outdoors. One of the reasons why I have never been a great fan of wearing iPods when running is because they limit my union with what is happening around me not to mention the reduction in one's safety awareness. Sometimes I have failed to dress and prepare enough for activities in the great outdoors. In two marathons in cold sunny spring weather, I got sunburnt because I failed to realise the strength of the sun and did not use a cap or put on sun-cream. I have got blisters, cramp and pulled the odd muscle because I wore the wrong socks, did not put on enough layers of clothing or wore clothing made of the wrong material for the conditions.

One has to be far more prepared for long runs than shorter ones. In training, you can nearly always cut your run short if weather conditions turn against you but this option is not open to you in a marathon. For longer runs when it is cold and possibly wet, I wear several layers of clothing with my favourite Helly Hanson being the first layer. The outer layer normally is a sleeveless wind jacket and I like to have a bum bag to store odds and ends. If it is just cold and dry in a race I wear the HH and a running vest for the race number. If I get too hot, off comes the HH to be wrapped round my waist with the added advantage of keeping my kidneys nice and warm. My biggest fear is getting wet feet early on in a long run or race. It is not a very pleasant experience to run with crinkly blistering feet for two or three hours. I can remember running in a downpour in one London marathon; but luckily, it happened near the Tower of London only about 8 km from the finish. In fact, I found the rain a welcome relief and it took my mind away from thinking about 'the wall'. Yes, there is no such thing as bad weather; still my shoes and socks were completely soggy at the finish but thankfully no blisters.

My ideal running surface is on grass or gravel pathways and if I have to run on tarmac, I prefer a road with a decent camber to avoid puddles of water. In very wet weather, the grass surface can become very soft and one risks, in my case at least, pulling an Achilles tendon. This happened to me when I was working at Mill Hill Public School in north London. This school has a great cross-country course, which includes some challenging hills and a stretch across a large cricket ground in a valley. Unfortunately, autumn 2000 was a very wet one and the cricket field became a bit bog-like but I failed to take account of this in trying to run a quicker training time and ended up with a very sore and stiff Achilles tendon. These sorts of injuries are hard to shift and four weeks later, I had to run the Lisbon marathon still with the tendon problem.

My dream weather for long distance running is a temperature around 5C to 10 C, dry and partially cloudy with a light variable breeze. However, for shorter runs I have enjoyed running in Norway at minus 10C on crunchy new snow. If it is snowing, I wear goggles as I find the snowflakes hurt my eyeballs. I wear a nice woolly hat, gloves and long johns with leggings and enjoy every minute of the run. I once did a training run on snow at minus 10C in Austria with some gentle slopes at an altitude of about 1000m and found it difficulty to breath, which resulted in a severe bout of coughing up of phlegm even up to an hour after the run. This was not a good idea. The following day I took a flatter course and a slower pace with a much better result. It is important to acclimatise when running at higher altitudes especially if you are getting on in years.

I have run at 30C in lovely sunshine in the south of France and as long as I did not exceed about 10Km or run too fast, found the training run immensely enjoyable. Some of my most memorable runs have been along the coast of Normandy, the hilly coastal paths of Brittany or up and down the beeches of Norfolk with a little bit of sand dune running but careful not to overstretch those Achilles tendons. Even in a big city, there are places to enjoy a good training run. When I worked at St Pauls School, I used the Thames river footpaths, which stretch for miles or Hampstead Heath where I did my first runs when I came over from Ireland.

The one place where I do not like running is on treadmills in Gyms. Yes, I know they are pretty girls to look at going through their paces but there is more of the fair sex running out on the open roads these days. hat better sight could there be than being left in the slipstream of a fair maiden as she glides past you with her hair flowing in the breeze—weather permitting of course!

THE BOSTON EXPERIENCE

I dedicate my 97th and 100th Boston Marathons to the memory of those who were killed and injured in The Terrorist attack on the marathon in April 2013.

Only qualifiers need apply

12M 97TH BOSTON MARATHON 19TH APRIL 1993

AT START OF 97TH BOSTON MARATHON 1993

Patriot's Day in Boston but it was no tea party for me

I had set my sights on running the Boston marathon soon after I completed my first marathon in 1984. The race at this time was only open to club members who achieve a specific qualifying time for their age and gender within the year prior to the marathon. This restricted the field to about 8000 runners in 1993. The qualifying time for me was to get less than 3hr 25 min in a recognised marathon and I managed to achieve this when I ran the 1992 London marathon in 3hr 23 min.

The Boston marathon is the world's premier road running event and is America's oldest annual sporting event. The marathon has been organised by the Boston Athletic Association since 1897. Scottish settlers, who brought with them the traditions of the highland games, founded the BAA in the middle of the 19th century.

The BAA mainly represented the United States at the first modern Olympics in Athens in 1896. Impressed by the running of the marathon in Athens, they set about organising one in Boston based on a similar type of course. The marathon course is from west to east, starting in the town of Ashland, then through the Newton Hills near Harvard University, across the Charles River and finishing in down—town Boston.

The first marathon was on Patriot's Day, Monday 19th April 1897 starting at 12.15pm with 15 runners. Ten runners finished the 25-mile course and John McDermott won the race in a time of 2hr 55minutes. Some of the many thousands of spectators present along the course placed bets on who would win the race.

The Boston marathon has had an individual winner each year since 1897 with the exception of 1918 when a relay event between the army and navy took place. This was due to American involvement in the First World War. All entrants to the Boston marathon must achieve a qualifying time in a recognised marathon in the year prior to the race.

In 1972, the first official women's Boston marathon took place and in 1979 Grete Waitz of Norway achieved the women's world record in a time of 2hrs 27 minutes. Joan Benoit of the United States set a new world record in 1983. Her time was 2hr 22minutes. The following year at the first women's Olympic marathon in Los Angeles, Benoit won the gold medal.

As well as the prestige of running at Boston, I had other reasons for selecting this particular marathon. The charity I was running for – The Thomas Coram Foundation – had links with the Boston area. The sea captain Thomas Coram who founded his Foundling Hospital by Royal Charter in London in 1742 had worked as a shipwright in the town of Taunton about 40 miles from Boston in the early 1700s. The house where he lived still stands today and the local church – St Thomas – has a stained glass window depicting the good captain in saintly pose. I managed to visit the church on Sunday the day before the marathon and got some generous sponsorship from the congregation. Also at this time I had a first cousin Glenda living in the Boston area who generously hosted me for all of my stay. My sister Avril also came down especially from Canada for the occasion.

As it has done for nearly a century, The Boston Athletic Association welcomed the running world to the 97th running of the Boston marathon on Patriot's Day Monday 19th April. The Marathon drew 8930 qualifying competitors (of whom 7517 finished) from 55 countries. There has been one British winner in 1970. Ron Hill ran a course record of 2 hours 10 minutes 30 seconds. In those days, they ran for prestige and not for money. The Boston marathon had difficulties in recruiting world-class runners in the 1980s because of competition from the emergence of big city marathons; but its future as the world's premier marathon was assured by an investment of several million dollars from the John Hancock Financial Services.

Normally well over a million spectators line the route and the runners get a very special welcome at 'Heartbreak Hill'. This comes at around the 18-mile mark and is a long upward incline of over half a mile. In 1993 there was a very special welcome for all the runners from the Boston marathon legend, John 'The Elder' Kelley. John Kelley started the Boston marathon 61 times, finished 59 times, won it twice and finished second on seven occasions. He represented the USA at the 'Hitler' Berlin Olympics in 1936. His last Boston marathon, at the age of 85 years, was the previous year 1992 and for the 97th running he ran the last 10km from the new sculpture titled ' Young at Heart' which had been unveiled just before the start of the Marathon in his honour at the foot of Heartbreak Hill. He died at the age of 97 in 2004. Not quite as famous is his namesake, was John J 'The Younger' who ran the Boston marathon on 32 occasions, winning it once and was second 5 times. He represented the USA at the Melbourne and Rome Olympics. Both of the Kelleys are represented in the runners 'Hall of Fame'.

The race started at mid-day and the weather was hot and sunny with a temperature in the mid 20s Celsius. The first few miles were slightly down hill on a narrow road in a field made more crowded by hundreds of unofficial runners. The good weather enabled the spectators to picnic with friends and added by a few beers give some very vocal support to the runners. In terms of noise, nothing beats the roar of the girl students at Wellesley College, alma mater of Hilary Clinton and Madeline Albright. The girls as usual were out in force and just about left enough room for the runners to get through, although the risk of eardrum perforation was very high. There was very little shade and my cotton-running vest increased in weight as it collected more of my perspiration. After a struggle through the Newton hills near Harvard University, it was a relief to run down to the Charles Bridge and cross over into down town Boston. I still remember with some pain the final long stretches along the Boston streets to the finish.

I only discovered how badly sunburnt I was when I emerged myself in a hot bath at the luxurious Boston Plaza Hotel when I wondered why the backs of my legs and neck were stinging with pain. There was going to be no shower or bath for me at all.

I met up my relatives at the 'Black Shamrock Pub', had a Boston Chowder fish soup with a few beers, and then headed out to Logan airport for a Virgin Atlantic early evening departure to London. When I got to the airport and checked in I was then told the flight was cancelled due to the pilot having food poisoning. This meant that I would not be able to go to work the next morning and the airline arranged for us to stay in the Boston Plaza Hotel. As I already had taken Monday off work I knew some of my colleagues would not be too pleased with their deputy head having more time off. The Boston marathon is a west to east afternoon race so the sun can be on the backs of the runners for several hours. Boston is the same latitude as Barcelona so in mid-April the sun can be very strong even though there can be still snow on the ground. Therefore, I learnt my lesson the hard way – next time use plenty of factor 40-suntan cream.

When I got back to school, I gave an assembly on my Boston marathon experience, which was well received by pupils and staff. Later I was able to present the director of The Thomas Coram Foundation with a large cheque when he came to the school.

20M 100TH BOSTON MARATHON

RUNNING THE WORLD'S OLDEST MODERN MARATHON FOR THE WORLD'S OLDEST INCORPORATED CHARITY.

BOSTON MARATHON
April 19, 1993
Marathon Foto

AT FINISH OF 97TH BOSTON MARATHON RUNNING NO 7401

Whilst I achieved the qualifying time for the 97th Boston I failed to qualify for the 100th Boston marathon. I had targeted 2 marathons, Helsinki and Reims, to try to run the qualifying time of under 3hr 25 min for my gender and age (age 50 years at the time). The closest I got to this was 3hr 32 min in Reims. So how did I get to run the 100th Boston?

Three years previously an English sports company ' Sports Tour' offered 500 places to previous successful Boston entries if they went with that company to the US and paid an initial non-returnable deposit. I took up the offer as an insurance policy fully believing that I would qualify in my own right. I failed, so had to eat some humble American Pie and go with the sports company.

The normal field for Boston is about 9000 but for the 100th running, an exception was made and the field was upped to 40,000, the largest marathon in history and I believe that is the case today. It would still be the same course—a single one road start at Hopkinton-, which was the main reason for restricting the race entry to 9000 in the first place. The solution was to provide each runner with an electronic chip that would record individual times from crossing the start line and at other points along the course. In this way, they could stagger the start and control the flow of the race according to each runner's predicted finishing time. In my case it took me 26 minutes to get to the starting line after the official starting time.

It was an honour to be part of this historic occasion, one of America's oldest sporting events. Along the marathon course, we have several reminders of the creation of modern America. We have: Harvard University, MIT, Boston University, Wellesley College, The Boston Celtics, The Red Socks and Boston Bay clam powder soup. We have the place where Paul Reveres did his famous horse ride to signal the start of the revolutionary war of independence. We have the old established WASP banking families and we have the descendants of famine Irish and poor southern Italians. Above all, we have the Boston Marathon.

The sports company had booked us into the Boston Plaza Hotel which was the one where I had a free night's stay thanks to Virgin Atlantic Airlines when I ran the 97th Boston. The marathon was run, as usual ,on the third Monday in April—state holiday and Patriot's Day in the Commonwealth of Massachusetts. Once more I was running for the Thomas Corum Foundation of London charity. The race was due to start at noon but there was the logistical problem of getting some 40000 runners the 25 miles from central Boston out to the start. The solution was simple—use the famous American yellow school buses, about 850 of them.

I was up at 5.00am and was in the queue for my bus by 8.00am. American school buses are very basic in design and I had a very crowded and bouncy, twisting ride out to the start and at times I felt I was in a yellow submarine rather than a bus. There was some compensation from the comaradie and banter of fellow runners on the bus.

The weather was cool, fine and sunny. There were still large heaps of snow around, but the sun can be quite strong at this latitude in mid April and unlike my previous Boston run, I had plenty of factor 40 suntan cream to hand.

After waiting for at least two hours and to great emotional relief we finally got going with the world's press and TV there to record the occasion. Not alone did we have 40000 official runners but we were joined along the narrow course by an estimated unofficial 10000 other runners. Unless you are a front runner, the Boston marathon is not the best venue to achieve a PB and it is a hilly course. Just a mile or so into the run I observed one male runner getting a little too close to some small rocks at the edge of a wood adjacent to the road, he tripped, fell and hit his head on one of the rocks and was out cold. Several runners and spectators stopped to help but sadly for him his race was over.

In a crowded field it is best to just go with the flow and not to expend unnecessary energy trying to work your way through the field. There is time to do that later when the field thins out a bit. I saw a middle-aged blond woman running in shorts imprinted with the Swedish flag. Needless to say I was not going to miss the opportunity to introduce myself – in poor Norwegian—which she understood. She was born in America. Her parents had emigrated from Sweden and, like many Americans, was proud of her European roots. We ran together for about 5 miles. The part of the race that I was looking forward to, strange as it may seem, was heartbreak hill at the 19 mile mark. When we reached heartbreak hill I was delighted to see again the great 61 times Boston marathon runner ' John Kelley' standing right next to his own monument built in time for the 97th Boston Marathon encouraging the runners to do their best. This time I coped with the hill by reducing my stride, leaning forward and with fantastic crown support made it all the way to the top non-stop.

The next 'high' point of the course was Wellesley College for Girls and unlike in 1993 I was ready for the traditional high-pitched reception from the young women. Like the first occasion, I ran the gauntlet through a narrow channel to a crescendo of deafening screams. This was a real wake up call. Never have I looked down so many mouths and at so many tonsils before or since. The Wellesley roars—or screams—is a truly uplifting experience and a real tonic at such a key stage in the race. We left the Newton Hills and Cambridge to come down and across the Charles River into downtown Boston. The last few long wide streets can be tough going but I was pleased to finish even though it was my slowest time so far. But what a great occasion it was. My marathon certificate records that 'Sean A O'Reilly has successfully completed the100th running of the Boston Marathon in 3hr 52 min 05 sec' and that is good enough for me.

WITH SISTER AURIL AFTER 100TH BOSTON MARATHON IN 1996

After the race I joined my cousin and my sister down from Toronto in a very well appointed flat in a skyscraper over-looking the marathon finish area. As I sat down to a sandwich and Budweiser—what else would you drink in America?—I could see runners still finishing down below. By now the temperature had dropped and one felt sorry for the fun runners, sometimes including myself, who can take 2 to 3 hours longer than the elite runners to complete the course and are therefore more exposed to changing weather conditions and all the problems that can result. It sometime becomes not just a running ordeal but also a fight to survive heat stroke or hypothermia or a drenching depending on the weather of course.

The day after the marathon it poured with rain and the Gods must have been with us on marathon day.

Before I flew out to London in the late afternoon, I had time for a little shopping. A pair of jeans, some quality leather shoes and a present for my long-suffering wife were my priorities. In the pouring rain I wore a long leather jacket and walked slightly leaning forward as is my style. As I walked past a local church I noticed to my left a queue of poorly dressed people outside the church door. As I looked forward again, a man was standing right in front of me. He waved quickly some form of identification and said he was from the police department .He accused me of trying to pass drugs to the people in the queue. He was aggressive, in his mid-forties and looked tired around the eyes. He demanded that I come along with him and get into an unmarked white van some 20yards away. I said' no way' and then he accused me of having a gun, pointing at my jacket breast pocket and demanded I get it out. I slowly raised my right hand to my pocket as he watched intently and pulled out my camera, which he grabbed immediately. He looked at it and then told me to empty my pockets. Out came slowly my marathon medal and my purse. I now had my first chance to tell the purpose of my trip and that I was not the local drug trafficker but he still maintained his aggressive stance and still wanted to get me into the van. I was now regaining my composure and no way was I getting into that van. Reluctantly he gave back my camera and let me go. I walked about 50 yards and entered the first cloths shop I saw. Whilst looking at some jeans, there he was again demanding to look at my camera again. There were some British people near by but I felt terrible isolated – just this person and me. Eventually he gave me back my camera and departed. Welcome to America I thought. I have been on many marathon trips in foreign places on my own and experienced few problems apart from the odd theft or double charging deal. Still it is nice to have safety in numbers sometimes. I have certainly come to understand and sympathize with the problems many women can experience in big cities at night even in their own countries.

On a more cheerful note, I raised a considerable sum of money and was again able to present a cheque at my school a few days later to the director of The Thomas Coram Foundation; the world's oldest incorporated charity supporting young vulnerable children and their mothers in the greater London area.

> *"Overtraining is the biggest problem for runners who lack the experience or discipline to cope with their own enthusiasm"*
>
> Marty Liquori

FIVE MORE LONDON MARATHONS:
1988,1989,1992,1994,1998

M3 MY 2ND LONDON MARATHON 1988

No money from the tooth fairy

It was to be four years until I ran my next London marathon in 1988, but it was not for the want of trying. I applied for London in 1985 and 1987 but was rejected. My luck was in for 1988 and again I ran for a charitable cause. This was for 'The Anthony Nolan Bone Marrow Appeal', which had been set up by the mother in honour of her son Anthony who had recently died of Leukaemia. She wanted funds to set up a national and then international database to match possible bone marrow donors. I am pleased to state that in 2014 the charity is still in existence and there has been spectacular progress made in the treatment of childhood leukaemia. In the 1970s, the illness was nearly always fatal and death occurred within months of contracting the illness; but now three out of four children with the illness are cured. I ran the marathon in a T-Shirt provided by the charity in order to give maximum publicity for this very worthy cause.

Race day was cloudy but dry and shorts and T-Shirt were for me my main running attire, although the cotton T-Shirt did collect a lot of sweat especially around my lower back, which was not very pleasant. Nowadays I wear a sweat wicking elasticised running vest, which is a lot more comfortable. I cannot remember much of the race itself except that it had the unique inspiring London atmosphere and the usual abundance of runners in fancy dress. There was still the bleak stretch at Canary Wharf, which now was a large building site with few spectators. On looking back, I was surprised that I only achieve a time of 3hr 27 min despite looking remarkable fit and slim in the finishing photograph. I do have one very specific memory after the finish.

Sponsorship is very important to big city marathons. The London Marathon has had several major sponsors including: Gillette 1981-83, Mars 1984-88, ADT 1989-92, NutraSweet 1993-95 and Flora 1996-2009. Gillette sponsorship in 1981 was for £75000 and the new sponsors Virgin for 2010-2014 is for £17 million. The need to attract and pay top runners has added to the costs, but one hopes that a sizeable amount of the sponsorship goes towards the organisation of the marathon and to elected charities. The reward for me for running the 1988 Mars London Marathon was a mars—bar! Unsurprisingly I felt hungry after my exertions—no energy drinks or bananas in 1988—so I took a good bite from the mars—bar. This resulted in my front crown tooth ending up lodged in the remaining part of the mars—bar. It turned out to be a very costly mars—bar, as I had to have private dental care to repair the damage—the NHS was not into dental cosmetics in those days – just fillings and extractions.

The marathon bug had caught me and in the years that followed, I was to run at least one marathon a year and the world had became my stage on which I was to play out my running exploits.

M6 MY 3ʳᴰ LONDON MARATHON 1989

HALAHLUA H Running for the Thomas Coram Foundation

(formerly The Foundling Hospital, London)

In April 1988 I took up a new post at Ashlyns Upper School, Berkhamsted as Deputy Headmaster. This school and its 35 acre site was formerly The Thomas Coram Foundling Hospital which moved from Bloomsbury, London in the 1920s to Berkhamsted which ceased to be an orphanage in the early 1950s with the foundation of the NHS. It carried on its work with deprived children and single parent mothers in and around the London area. Some of the original buildings in Bloomsbury form part of the modern Coram Foundation. Ashlyns School has links with the foundation and supports some of its charity work but surprisingly as the world's and London's oldest incorporated charity with a Royal Charter from 1739 it was not involved with the London marathon. That was to change when I contacted the Director and offered to run the marathon in support of the Foundation. The Foundation over the years raised funds from private benefactors and from the annual performances of Handel's Messiah, who had donated the performance rights to the Foundation in the 18C. In 1989 they still took minutes of their meetings using a quill pen; but the appointment of a new Director brought their funding raising methods into the twentieth century.

As usual the atmosphere and the occasion was very uplifting and motivating. Suffice to quote from my local paper: 'Top marks at Ashlyns School this week went to Deputy Head Mr Sean O'Reilly after his third London Marathon. Mr O'Reilly (42) completed the run in 3hr 25 min and his medal was proudly displayed at school on Monday morning. He is raising money which will be donated to the Thomas Coram Foundation for their London Children in Need campaign. The school was originally the Thomas Coram Foundling Hospital and the organisation is this year celebrating its 250th anniversary.'

M10 MY 4ᵀᴴ LONDON MARATHON 1992

A Choice to make.

Eight years after my first London marathon, I was pleased to achieve one of my better finishing times of 3hr 23 min finishing with a sprint to the finishing line on Westminster Bridge. This time I was using the London marathon to try to qualify for the world's most famous and oldest modern marathon, namely the US Boston Marathon. For my gender and age, I needed a time of 3hr 25min or less within one year of the next running of the Boston marathon. I just made it by 2 minutes and so I would be on my way to run the 97ᵗʰ Boston marathon the following April.

As with all big city marathons I was keen to run for a worthy charitable cause, and this time the choice of charity came down to two, both provided by my two son's medical schools. My choice was reported in my local paper as follows: 'Ashlyns School, Berkhamsted, is putting its money on deputy headmaster Sean O'Reilly for the running of his fourth London marathon. Mr O'Reilly's two sons are both medical students – one at The Royal Free Hospital, London and one at Guy' Hospital, London and both hospitals were seeking marathon sponsorship for their charitable projects. Mr O'Reilly had a loyalty problem when it came to selecting which one to support. In the end he opted for Guy's Hospital new kidney donor unit and specialists cots for premature babies appeal. The Royal Free Hospital was an appeal for a capital project to build another floor for the medical school. By way of explanation, he feels that it is the responsibility of the Government to provide funding for capital projects. Charity should be for the extra icing on the cake as it were. I managed to collect over £500 for Guys a good sum of money in 1992 and I still have my Guy's Hospital mug as a memento of my sponsorship.

The marathon itself lived up to its usual wonderful atmosphere enhanced by fine weather. I had a comfortable run and even had some energy left over, so much so that only one hour after the race I took a train from Liverpool Street station to Harwich to join my wife and daughter on the Ferry boat to Sweden. I can still remember the good few beers that I had with some Scottish Golf Coaches on their way to Sweden for the summer golf season. They were quite impressed with my very up to date London marathon T—shirt which was just a few hours old.

M15 MY 5ᵀᴴ LONDON MARATHON APRIL 1994

I dedicate this Marathon to the memory of Kieran Jones

A nephew on the run

By 1994 The London Marathon was big news with up to 30,000 runners and more than twice that number rejected. The race now had two main start areas in Blackheath and Greenwich with a red start for the fun runners and a blue start for the Elite runners and a green start for women over 60 and men over 65—maybe something to look forward for me in a couple of years! The elite women runners started at 9.00 followed by the rest at 9.30. The finish was now in The Mall in front of Buckingham Palace and every mile was marked by an arch of coloured balloons and drinks stations – sheer luxury since my first London marathon in 1984.

During the night before this marathon Kieran Jones, a former soldier and a local police officer at that time from Gravesend, Kent, ran the marathon course in full military kit with backpack for charity. He had failed to get an entry to the marathon but he was still determined to run the course. His friend Arturo Gonzales provided a support vehicle and helped Kieran through parts of the marathon course on foot that were closed until the morning – Tower of London and Canary Wharf to name but two. Arturo had at times to run with Kieran to guide him onto the line marking the marathon course. They arrived at the finish in front of Buckingham Palace around 6 am. They had covered several kilometers more than the 42.2 km marathon course. Later on hearing about their feat, I was able to present Arthuro with a spare London marathon medal that I got when I finished the 'official' marathon later in the day. He is now back living in his native Spain. Kieron went on to achieve other marathon successes but sadly died a few years later.

Despite the different starts, it was still very crowded for the first 8 miles or so until well past the Cutty Sark. I was hoping to get under 3.30 but it would have been very unwise to try and push through the field because of the excess energy needed. Better to go with the flow and soak up the atmosphere of this unique marathon.Besides I did not want to have to push past too many Elvis Presley's, bears or Viking ships too early in the race. It was a cold day for late April but ideal for marathon running and for those dressed up as furry animals.

This marathon was notable because my 20-year-old nephew Adrian Horgan was running and achieved a very commendable time of 3hr 36 min. We never met up during the race—almost impossible with so many participants—but I finished in 3hr 34min which was satisfactory for me and more importantly I collected over £500 for The Thomas Coram Foundation. The Foundation had now got its act together and had 3 other sponsored runners in the race – 2 Coldstream Guards and an employee. Again I had good support from my colleagues and pupils at my school who as usual showed a keen interest in my marathon endeavours. The excellent media coverage of The London Marathon even gets some of them out of bed on Sunday morning to see the start on TV.

M26 MY 6ᵀᴴ LONDON MARATHON 1998

FINISHING LONDON MARATHON 1998 RUNNING NO 3086

Arslan gets his moment in Narnia

Some people try to run the London every year or as many times as possible over a lifetime, but I have always taken the view that in a very oversubscribed marathon others should be given a chance to participate. I like different challenges both in Britain and abroad. Experience has shown than all marathons have their own unique atmosphere and course organisation. Occasionally I run the same city marathons more than once: London, Dublin, Boston and Antwerp; but as a rule I prefer to run in cities or countries that I have not run in before. This marathon was very special for me because it was the first time that one of my students participated in the race.

Arslan was a final year student at my school and was born in England of Pakistani parents. He was a member of Chesham Cricket Club and played to school county standard. Cricket was his first sporting love so it was a surprise when he came and asked me about running a marathon. Normally I do not encourage young people to run marathons until well into their late twenties; but to first enjoy and experience track or cross country running up to 10km or half-marathon distances. Arslan applied for entry to the London Marathon and was very disappointed when he was rejected—even more so when I told him that I had been accepted. I felt somewhat sorry for him as I was very impressed by his general sporting intelligence, enthusiasm and ability. As luck would have it, I had already encouraged The Thomas Coram Foundation to apply for gold entries as one of London's oldest charities and they still had one entry available on condition that a good sum of money was raised in sponsorship for their charity. One phone call to the Foundation secured a place for Arslan to his delight so we would both run the marathon and for the same charity. I was particular pleased with Arslan's participation because few people of Pakistani or Indian origin participate in long distance running but instead they prefer to excel at cricket, squash and hockey in particular. I am sure that this will change in the years ahead.

My preparation for this marathon was unusual with my longest run of about 14 miles in a semi blizzard in Norway two weeks before the marathon. The place where I stayed and skied was near Geilo at an altitude of about 800meters. My runs were confined to running up or down a valley with very few level paths. Thermals and goggles were essential but I was lucky that the snow was well below zero and powder in form rather than wet snow with chunks of ice. At times I did have to contend with a cold blast of wind coming down the valley but again this was nothing compared to what the great arctic Norwegian explorers Nansen and Amundsen had to contend with. A few days later I descended from the mountains and went to my wife's home town of Harmar in east Norway and the home to skating for the 1992 Winter Olympics. Here I got a few 10km runs in on a flat frozen lake and then back to London three days before the start of the London marathon. In fact I was in quite good shape as I got in a few weeks averaging 25 miles per week and training at altitude was a bonus. One great Norwegian runner Ingrid Christiansen lived in north Norway and did a lot of training on snow as well as the treadmill when it was too cold outside and yet she was able to come in April to London and win the marathon in 1984.

A great positive for me now was that I had finally given up cigars with the aid of hypnosis and shear willpower, but I still had a few too late pub sessions. However, I did restrict myself to only 2 pints of Guinness at a friend's 50th birthday party the night before the marathon and was up at 6.30 am to enjoy my Quaker's porridge breakfast and after a good rub of Vaseline in the right places I put on my running kit and drove down to near Trafalgar Square, parked up and caught the 8.10 am train from Charing Cross to Greenwich. The train was crowded with fellow runners and we all enjoyed the great banter between us. I managed to talk to two American girls from the lone star state who had run the US Texas Austin marathon the previous year and London would be their second marathon. I also talked to a lady in her 50s who was running her first ever marathon for a Cancer charity who needless to say was very nervous but excited by the whole occasion—even if she had to stand up in the crowded train .

As usual the London marathon had great spectator support with lots of razzmatazz and fancy dress runners in all sorts of garb. The weather was kind to us and I was able to run in running vest and shorts with my usual Nike socks and shoes. There was a bit of a downpour near the Tower of London so my shoes were a bit squashy for the last few miles. My time of 3hr 45 m was in line with my expectations and previous training schedule.

I did not see my pupil Arslan during the race but he completed his first ever marathon in 3hr 55min which was a very respectable time. Between us we raised about £2000 for The Thomas Coram Foundation. Other teachers and students from the school were to follow our example and run the London Marathon in support of the Foundation. I often wonder what became of Arslan.

"Three Quarks for Mister Mark and sure any he has are all beside the mark"

James Joyce, Finnigan's Wake

IN DUBLIN'S FAIR CITY

5M DUBLIN MILLENNIUM MARATHON OCT 1988

No Viking Invasion this time

My fifth marathon was to find me back in the city where I was born in 1946 – Dublin. The marathon was part of the celebrations For the founding of Dublin by the Vikings in 988 or thereabouts. Most of the Vikings that invaded Ireland were I believe from Norway and as my wife is from Norway I decided to leave her back in London as I was not sure if the Irish could cope with another Viking evasion.

My trip was organised by a fairly amateurish but keen Irish tour company and after a grand tour of the suburbs of Dublin in a minibus. I was dropped off at a B&B in the northern suburbs of the city a very long walk from the city centre. Luckily, I was to be collected on the morning of the marathon by said minibus. On the Saturday, I arranged to meet up with an old school friend from near Kells in County Meath as well as some friends on a tour of Ireland who were from Maidstone in Kent. We ended up in a Church Parish Club and I confined myself to four pints of Guinness and four Hamlet cigars and thankfully my Irish friend got me back to my B&B not long after midnight.

At this point, I must confess to my cigar addiction. I have never been a committed cigarette smoker; but I did like to have a small cigar when having a beer or two. Unfortunately, I got to the stage where I could not enjoy a pint without a cigar. Eventually my main motivation for going to the pub was to get my hands on a cigar as I was determined never to smoke at home or buy a packet of cigars in a shop. I knew that I was in trouble when I finished the cigar before my pint of beer and inhaled more with each successive pint. I used to wake up in the night feeling depressed by my excesses and with a throat as rough as a camel's arse. It was only after hypnosis by my Dentist and in his dental chair of all places that I finally kicked the habit some ten years later. I do not think that my smoking or drinking habits effected my marathon times too much, although I did give up both for six months before my first marathon and did achieve my best marathon time ever; but my training programme was much more demanding then than in subsequent marathons.

After a good Irish feed of porridge for breakfast my friend 'the minibus ' picked me up and dropped me off in O'Connell Street for the start of the marathon at 9.30am. The course was a figure of eight shape .We ran the south loop first past Trinity College and into the well-heeled Lansdowne and Ballsbridge areas and then the north loop past the Gaelic football ground of Croke Park and on into urban north Dublin. Croke Park witnessed an invasion by elements of the British army during the war of independence in 1920 when they opened fire on the players and spectators killing one player and several spectators. This attack was a response to the assignation of the Cairo ring of British secret agents earlier in the day. Some years later, I ran past another football stadium in Santiago, Chile, which was the scene of a far greater slaughter of civilians and politicians by then Chilean dictator General Pinochet. I am pleased to state that some years later; Queen Elizabeth the Second visited the stadium in a spirit of reconciliation.

Dublin marathon is always run on the last Monday in October, which is a national holiday and the weather is ideal for marathon running as long as it does not rain and even if it does it tends to be only of the drizzle sort or what we call Irish Mist. This particular marathon was well supported with spectators well spread around the course. I have two distinct memories from this marathon.

Firstly, I was nearly beaten to the finish by a man quite a few years older than me whose race plan seemed to be sprint, walk, sprint and walk over most of the course. Each time I passed him, as he walked, at my steady running pace of just over 5 minutes per kilometre I thought that would be the last I saw of him but alas a few minutes later he would sprint past me again. I have to say I admired his tenacity but I did find him extremely irritating to say the least. It soon became a separate target for me to finish ahead of him which I did—but it was a real struggle to the very end. I have never ceased to be amazed by the different styles of running and the physical shapes of both men and women who run marathons. I have seen runners very knocked kneed, bow legged, raising their heels so that they almost touched the small of their back, leg actions like flippers but they all still complete their marathons. At times, I am surprised that some of them can walk never mind run. My finishing time of 3 hr 26 min was not too bad for me in 1988.

My second memory is the Gay Baths that my travel company had organised for us to use after the race. The shower water was cold and the water in the small pool was even colder but did not stop the local naked men being very friendly to the few runners who dared to use these facilities. My Irish friend was very surprised that my travel company had chosen the 'Gay Baths' for us. Anyway, marathon running is certainly not an aphrodisiac and cold showers never did turn me on.

Afterwards I met up with my fan club for a few more Guinness and then it was 'time up' when my 'minibus' friend arrived

25M DUBLIN MARATHON 1997

Come back Sean O'Reilly to Ballyjamesduff.

It was nine years since my last marathon in the fair city and this time I organised the weeklong trip myself so that I could stay with my Irish friend from my school days and with my first cousin Patrick up in Dundalk. On this occasion, my daughter Astrid came with me on only her second trip to the Emerald Isle. On later trips abroad, she would join me to run as well. One of the highlights of the trip was a visit to my father's birthplace in Ballyjamesduff, County Cavan. There is a well-known Irish song by Percy French called 'Come back Paddy Reilly to Ballyjamesduff'; well this time it was Sean O'Reilly who was coming back.

We arrived on Saturday for the usual Monday start of the marathon on a very cold late damp misty October day. Halloween was due and I expected some Critereens , Gobbeens or even the odd Banshee to jump out of the misty hedges on our way through the country side to my friend's local village. I was looking forward to a few pints of Irish brewed Guinness to lift my spirits as it were. In the local bar I delved into my first pint with gay abandon only to be shocked with how cold it was, almost freezing. Well I knew the evening was near to freezing but we were inside a fairly warm pub. My second pint was just as cold but by then I was beginning to be numbed by the alcohol but I still felt my stomach cramping up a bit. After four pints we decided to go back for dinner but before going I checked with the barman as to why the Guinness was so cold and he told me that I had been drinking the new super-cooled brand. On Sunday I compounded my mistake when I had another four pints of the freezing stuff at my friend's late father's local pub in Fordstown near Kells some 40 miles north of Dublin. There they did not have normal Guinness so I decided to give the extra cold stuff another chance. To this day, I have an aversion to any super-cooled or extra cold drink and besides it destroys the taste. Even on the Monday morning of the race, my stomach was still unsettled so it was only a bread and water marathon breakfast.

The course for this marathon was a single loop taking in the south and western part of the city. The weather was dull, cold and breezy and not too bad for long distance running. There was a large field of some 8000 runners in addition to a few hundred walkers mostly from America. The large number of Americans competing I believe was due to the strong links between Ireland and the Irish American Diaspora. Many of them were running for a charity to do with Leukaemia and they wore tee shirts with a picture and name of someone who had recently died from the disease – very moving. I was also impressed with the walkers who set out two hours before the marathon start and remained cheerful as we caught up with them. The crown support was poor compared to the Millennium Dublin marathon in 1988. In some ways, it was understandable as the Irish were celebrating a long weekend and an early rise on Monday morning was not one of their priorities.

The start and finish was as usual in O'Connell Street. Despite having the luxury of being dropped off near the start by my Irish friend, I still managed to forget my energy bars. I also lost about 5 minutes on the clock because of the single crowded start. There were no electronic chips to give you your real time back then. Things picked up a bit as we went past Trinity College, Ireland's oldest university and headed south past Lansdowne to the grounds of the National University College of Dublin. Luckily, I got talking to an American who generously gave me one of his energy gels. The number of spectators increased and I managed to keep running at a steady pace. The last four miles along the side of a wall enclosing the Phoenix Park – possible the world's largest capital city park—was hard work. The spring in my legs had gone by now and I was passed by an American girl who I had talked to earlier and by the American man who had given me the energy gel. The race providers only supplied water, luxuries like isotonic drinks and Bananas would have to wait until later marathons. I managed to run non-stop but I did learn that my decreasing pace might have been less so with a bit more carbohydrate loading before and during the race. Still I was pleased with my clock time of 3hr 42min.

I did notice the increase in the number of women runners since 1988. Of the 13 O'Reillys in the race 7 were women and two of these were from America. When I first came to London in 1960, I used to run along the streets to have a run round the beautiful and hilly Hampstead Heath and then run home again. I finished the experience by putting some pennies into the slot machine that controlled the gas heater for a nice hot bath. In those days, I never noticed any other joggers on the streets of London back then-I think people thought that I was a bit of an eccentric and after all why would anyone want to run when you could take a bus or the tube. I think that we have to be thankful to our American cousins for getting 'jogging' up and running as it were. Frank Shorter's marathon win for the US at the Munich Olympics in 1972 and the setting up of the New York Marathon a few years later captured the imagination of Americans and got some of them out to jog and this became a worldwide phenomena with the creation of other big city marathons. Despite the early marathon successes of the Norwegians Greta Weisz and Ingrid Christiansen and the first women allowed to run the Boston marathon, women were a little slower to take up jogging than men. The 1990s brought a boom in women's running and now whilst out for a jog I often see more women than men running. An additional inspiration for women is not only the body shaping benefit of running but also the health benefits in combating bone disease. They also have the benefit of safety in numbers when running in urban areas.

As it was half term my wife was on a study trip to Germany and my daughter and I were able to spend a few days visiting my childhood homelands in Ireland—Meath, Cavan and Louth – all to the north of Dublin. Most foreign tourists head for the south and west of Ireland and miss one of the wonders of the world – the Neolithic burial grounds at Newgrange and Knowth in County Meath – over a thousand years older than the Pyramids. They miss out the Cooley Hills and the lakes and drumlins of County Cavan. This part of Ireland is quite flat and has excellent grazing land. A poem (anon) about a drover I learnt at school comes to mind:

'To Meath of the pastures I lead my cattle and me

Through Leitrim and Longford I name them the byways which they are to pass without heed

To Meath of the pastures where there is grass to the knee and salt by the sea' Anon

Up until the early 1950s, young cattle were walked(droved) from the poor pasture land of Sligo and Mayo in the west of Ireland to be fattened up on the rich pastures of Meath on the east coast. As my Granny said to me on many occasions, 'where there is beauty in the landscape there is poverty'. Give me the green plains of Meath and the Hill of Tara every time.

NEW YORK NEW YORK

18M NEW YORK MARATHON 1994

A weekend to remember.

New York was the first of the modern big city marathons. The first marathon was a 5 lap course in Manhattan Central Park, but was then expanded to include the five main boroughs of the city. The new start was on Staten Island, crossing the 2-mile long Verrazano Bridge over the Hudson into Brooklyn. It then makes its way up through Brooklyn to Queens and then north into The Bronx and then south again to finish in Manhattan Central Park. I was pleased to be selected for a place in the 1994 silver anniversary running of the marathon.

A few years before when I visited New York, I met my wife's Norwegian uncle Odd. He had immigrated to the US just after the Second World War, following his father who had come to the US in the 1930s. He invited me back to be his guest if I decided to run the marathon. Time was running out for Odd as he was suffering from terminal bowel cancer and I was pleased to get over to New York when he still was in good enough health to show me around and share a few beers.

Early November is a very busy time for secondary schools in England. Autumn term is the main teaching term in the year without too many interruptions in terms of examinations and school visits and examiner's meetings. I was going to have to get out and back to New York without missing any school time. Unfortunately, there are very few marathons in the northern hemisphere in the school holidays so weekends it has to be for me.

At 4pm I packed my work suit away at school, put on my casual gear, grabbed my kit bag and off with a work colleague who dropped me at Heathrow in time for the 7pm flight to New York. In those days you did not have to get to the airport 3 hours before a transatlantic flight and security precautions were minimal.

The plane was only half-full and, as it was Friday evening a few drinks with some fellow passengers at the back of the plane were in order. In 1994 you could still smoke on planes, so I was able to have, secretly of course, a few of my favourite Hamlet cigars. I saw the light of day under hypnosis on my local dentist's chair in 1998 and thankfully have not smoked since. With all the free booze supplied by the air staff, I arrived in New Jersey well oiled and prepared for the night session in New York. I was met by my uncle Odd and his partner who then drove straight to the Norwegian Soccer Club in north Brooklyn It was not long before I was downing some more beer. This time I noticed that several generous customers were passing me Irish whiskeys, which I soon realised, was part of the city bar tradition whereby the customer buys two drinks and the barman buys you one back. By 1am New York time I was pleased when my uncle suggested we go back to his flat this time driven by his teetotal partner. My body clock time was 6am and I was exhausted. However, my uncle had other ideas.

Four hours later at about 6am I woke up to my uncle shouting that coffee was ready and the marathon Irishman had not come to New York to lie in bed all day, especially when we had a big city to see. As I was still well 'oiled' from the evening-night sessions the day before, I was up for it, well at least for the first two hours. We went out for a Brooklyn style fry up with two eggs for me sunny side-up and copious amounts of black coffee. On the way up to town to register for the marathon at the Hilton Hotel in Manhattan, Odd was keen to introduce me to his local – The Leaf Eriksen Bar. The Eriksen name for the bar was in honour of Leif Eriksen who could have been the first European to discover America. Incidentally Odd's surname was also Eriksen. The 'Leaf' part of the bar's name was to do with leaf as in Shamrock Leaf. The bar did have strong Irish-Norwegian connections. Most of the bar staff were young Irish men and women and most of the clients were older Norwegians, many of whom worked as tug pilots on the nearby Hudson Bay River. A couple of beers later, we went to the metro to go to Manhattan and on the way to the station we passed a vegetable shop. Odd asked me to name any of the vegetables on the display. I recognised some onions and carrots but that was all. It turned out that the shop was Vietnamese whose people were the latest addition to the 'melting pot' and who had brought their own range of vegetables to the new World. Brooklyn has been host to successive waves of immigrants: Dutch, German, Irish, Italian, Russian Jews, Scandinavians (known locally as square heads—according to my Norwegian uncle), Hispanics and many others. As each group prospered, they moved out to the richer suburbs and became commuters.

Up town we got to register at the huge Hilton Hotel and then my uncle took me up the Empire State building which his father had helped to build. This was followed by 5th Avenue, Times Square and a visit to a famous Irish Pub. By now I was feeling truly awful. I was unable to finish my Guinness and luckily my 70 year old uncle was flagging a bit and so it was to the metro and back the 12 odd miles to South Brooklyn and a quick visit again to The Leaf Eriksen and then the walk to his flat. By now, my stomach was really playing up due to my drinking excesses and often as a result I get an attack of stomach migraine—well that's my theory anyway. I was able to eat just a sandwich, so no carbohydrate loading this time and to bed by 9pm.

I was up again at 6 am on the Sunday morning, but this time for a good reason, as we had to get across the Verrazano Bridge before it closed for the marathon, which was going to start in Staten Island. Odd had prepared beef, ham and cheese sandwiches that were more appropriate for a worker going out to work all day on a building site, which he had done for many years. I struggled to his amazement to eat the sandwiches as my stomach was still somewhat raw, but managed to eat most of the bread for the carbohydrates if not the protein in the sandwich fillings.

The New York marathon starts at midday, thankfully for my sake as it gave me some more recovery time. Odd dropped me off at about 9am and gave himself enough time to get back across the bridge before it closed. The weather was a little warm—20C plus and humid for early November and I was able to lie down on the grass on parkland in the starting area. Several runners were getting married on a stage nearby and the announcers were speaking in different languages on the antennae. Gradually it all became a blur and soon I was oblivious to everything going on around me – I was fast asleep.

The next thing that I remember was been shaken and on looking up I saw a figure in a yellow tunic, silhouetted by bright sunshine, was I in the next world I thought? On second thoughts, no, I was not. The figure turned out to be not my redeemer offering me redemption but a park attendant offering me my last chance to run the New York marathon. 'Wake up man' he said 'You aint gonna run no marathon asleep, theys already gone man.' I sat up and sure enough they had gone, but I still had the presence of mind to rush to the toilet for a quick light relief, ran out of the park and on to the main highway. Ahead I saw some 25000 runners waiting on the rising slope of the bridge and within seconds cannons sounded off, ships on the Hudson Bay sounded their fog horns, helicopters hovered overhead; the 25th New York Marathon had started. It was difficult to believe that only two weeks after starting last in the Abingdon marathon in England that again I was the last runner to start this race.

With every step I took, I felt better and this was the case for almost the whole marathon. With every sip of water, I felt invigorated and life was worth living after all. My hangover was soon only a distant memory.

I decided to run on the lower tier of the bridge and half way across I noticed that it was raining; but on looking out onto the bay I could see a clear blue sky. The water was coming from the upper tier of the bridge and I soon realised that it was not rainwater but human urine. Yes, marathon running does strange things to runners and getting the runs before and during a race is one of them. Normally I am able to resist the urge, but others of a more nervous disposition cannot. It was ironic that I had spent the past 36 hours getting rid of my own urine from my binge drinking; now I had to cope with other people's urine. A quick move to the middle of the road found me in a much drier climate even if a bit more crowded.

I had arranged to meet my uncle and his band of supports about a mile beyond the bridge and soon I saw the Norwegian flags in the distance and within minutes, I was shaking hands with Odd and his many friends. I really was now on my way to Manhattan.

Whilst not as theatrical as the London marathon, New Yorkers are very gutsy in their support for the runners. Many runners had their first names printed on their running vests which allowed the spectators to call out their names with glee. Our Uncle Sam cousins just love to be on first name terms whether it is work or play in contrast to the more reserved Mr John Bull. As we passed through each of the Boroughs the ethnic mix of the spectators changed from a majority Asian in south Brooklyn, Hispanic in north Brooklyn , Hasidic Jew in Queens, African American in the Bronx and the full ethnic melting pot in Manhattan. The parts of the race that I found hard going were the long haul uphill to the Bronx and a steep incline at the entrance to Central park. I finished in a time of 3hr 39min, which given the humidity, jet lag, lack of sleep and myself imposed excesses, was a very satisfying time for me.

Post race I had the problem of trying to get the metro back to south Brooklyn. I was confused about up town and down town, where was the centre of town I thought? After a few runs on a shuttle train I got off and luckily remembered my uncle telling me to get a train numbered N57. I was still in my running gear apart from an extra sweat shirt and Pair of leggings when, I got to the Leif Eriksen where there was a very lively reception for me led by my uncle Odd of course. This time I restricted by self to just a couple of beers and gave my barman's free drink to another grateful customer. A walk back to Odd's flat followed by a very welcome quick hot bath and then the drive to Kennedy Airport. The plane was only half-full and I was able to strap myself in to three central seats and made a request to cabin staff only to wake me up when we got near to Heathrow.

We landed at 5.30am and my friend picked me up at 7pm to be in school by 8 am. After a quick shower, shave and change into my working suit, I was ready to take morning chapel assembly. I open my assembly with the words: 'Good morning pupils and staff, eleven and a half hours ago, I crossed the finish line in the 25th New York marathon'. The look of disbelief on the faces of the staff and pupils was something to behold; but teacher never lies and I hope they knew something about time zones.

Thank you uncle Odd for being a great host and may you sail happily in your Viking ship across the heavenly waters of Valhalla. **Yes, a weekend to remember!**

"Experience is the name every one gives to their mistakes"

Oscar Wilde

*"To survive to become an experienced marathon runner,
you must learn from your mistakes"*

The Author

FOUR FAMOUS BELGIAN MARATHONS

11M –BRUSSELS 1992, 13M – BERCHAM 1993, 23M – ANTWERP 1997, 29M —BELGIAN COAST 2007

Famous Belgians and not just chocolate

IN ANTWERP CENTRE WITH WIFE AND DAUGHTER

I have run four marathons in Belgium thanks in the main to the hospitality of a great Belgium friend, Jacques, from Antwerp. The four marathons run to date include : Brussels 1992, Berchem, Antwerp 1993, City of Antwerp 1997 and the Belgian Coastal Marathon 2007.

My wife and I met Jacques in Germany on one of our self-organised school trips to the Rhineland over 20 years ago. Jacques has never failed to join us on our annual school trips to Germany since. We like to think of him as our European Representative and we have been his guest in his home city of Antwerp on several occasions as he has been our guest in England – the country of birth of his father. Jacques's father was a British soldier in Belgium at the end of the Second World War where he met Jacques's Belgium mother and settled permanently there.

Many English people like to display their ignorance by asking 'How many famous Belgians can you name?' They think of course that they are very few; but fail to understand that Belgium only came into existence in 1831. Most of them do not realise that Belgium consists of Flemish and French speaking people as well as a German minority. The famous Flemish school of painting was based in Antwerp and includes Rubens and Van Dyke, yet they never are called Belgians. Ignorance is bliss for some people I guess. I have always found Belgium excellent value for money as well as being clean and efficient. It is not just their chocolates that tempt me, but also their food and massive range of beers. I can never understand why the Belgians are so generous in having most of their motorways with electric lighting and all are toll free compared to say France or Italy.

My first Belgium marathon was in Brussels and my wife and I were joined by Jacques and a neighbour of his from Antwerp. It was a one loop course with just 1km of the course two-way. I was surprised to find that there was quite a large hill and that the city itself had some challenging inclines and cobbled streets; but there was a nice balance between inner city streets and country parks. It was a very pleasant mid-September day with about 2000 runners participating.

I was pleased with a time of 3hr 27min and it was not long before we were back in Antwerp and I had my first Duval beer. My friends had told me that they had their own marathon in Antwerp – on the same day—but I did not know this when I booked my place for Brussels. It was clear to me that they would have preferred me to run their home town marathon and I was pleased to return the following year to run in their famous Flemish city with its ancient Napoleonic docks.

13M BERCHAM-ANTWERP MARATHON 1993

Like Brussels the previous year, the conditions for the marathon in September were excellent. This was the 24th running of the marathon and was unusual in that the start was in the centre of the city with the finish in the Berchem suburb. We were bussed into the centre for the start and got good support from my wife, daughter – who would later run a half-marathon in Belgium with me – and our Belgian friends.

The first stage of the race out of the city centre took us through the 'Diamond Area' and it was noticeable that there were many Orthodox Jews in the area and I can only presume that they were involved in the diamond business. Later we did visit the area to see how diamonds were cut and set into jewellery.

Once out of the centre we did two laps in the suburb of Berchem. I could not help but notice a strong chemical smell in the air – it certainly kept me alert. After all Antwerp has one of the largest industrial inland ports in Europe with an abundance of petro-chemical plants. There were only about a thousand runners in the race and it was motivating to be passed by the front runners and to see just how fast they moved compared with the main body of runners. I was very pleased with my finishing time of 3hr 21min – my best for nine years.

As usual we dined well that evening. Antwerp has many small family restaurants, not the chains of restaurants that we have in England. The family owners take pride in treating their customers well and it is customary to get a free aperitif and a complementary liquor and coffee at the end of the meal. I do not remember ever getting a complementary drink in an English restaurant. It was our Belgian friend Jacques who introduced my wife and me to the joy of eating Moules with chips and a garlic sauce and they now are part of our annual culinary treats, even when there is not an 'R' in the month. During our stay we enjoyed a meal with one of Jacques neighbours who cooked a very nice beef Wellington. On a later visit the same neighbour cooked one of the biggest chickens that I have ever seen. It was only when he started to carve the chicken that I realised that it had no inner hollow—it was a completely reconstructed chicken made up from at least three separate chickens. Still it tasted great and there was more than enough for everyone.

23M ANTWERP MARATHON 1997

I was to return to Antwerp for the 3rd running of the new city based marathon in April 1997 and again with my wife and daughter. By now, keeping to the same level of preparation I was finding it hard to break 3hr 30 min and finished in a time of 3hr 36 min. The race was sponsored by Lipton Iced Tea a Belgium's favourite drink but not quite as tasty as their beer.

29M BELGIAN COASTAL MARATHON 2007

Seven years on I again returned to Belgium this time with my daughter who would run the half marathon. The marathon was an unusual course along the Belgian coast and they would select the direction two days before to make sure the runners did not have to face a strong coastal headwind all the way. The direction selected was from Le Penne via Neuport to Oostende. It was surprising that Belgium could organise a coastal marathon in view of the fact that most of their coastline is built up with endless rows of sea front blocks of flats with the odd gap here and their. It is as if a large sea wall or dyke had been built along the coast. Still there were some nice long wide seafront promenades to run along and the flats formed only a narrow strip in places so it was possible to run on nice country paths a bit inland through fields with grazing cows.

We arrived in Antwerp with Euro Star via Brussels where we were hosted again by Jacques. On the Friday evening Jacques prepared a substantial pasta dish and afterwards we had a few Belgian beers in his local billiards club and were in bed by midnight. Up at 7.30 for a good breakfast of porridge and then Jacques drove us the 90-minute trip – a good chance for me to lie down in the back of the car for another rest—to Neuport the half way point of the marathon course. We registered at Neuport where Astrid started her half-marathon at 11am while Jacques and I drove to the start at La Penne. There were not many foreigners running but I did meet a man from Reading who hoped to do a PB of less than 3hr 30min. The weather was ideal for running: slight breeze, 15 Celsius and partly cloudy. This was the only marathon where I experienced a delayed start of about 15 minutes, understandable in view of the late decision on deciding in which direction to run the race. They race included several relay teams which added to the organisational complications.

As for the race itself, it was not a very crowded field but the relay runners can put one off one's pace a little and at other times, they can be an incentive to keep going. I got to halfway in 1hr 47min and that was a very good time for me. Then a nice run along a canal; but it got colder with some spitting rain and a strong crosswind. I decided to tuck in behind a small group of runners—a well used tactic of mine at this stage in a marathon—for a few kilometres, but some other runners in small groups came past which meant I was slowing down. I reached my key time targets of 2.20 (Hertford to Finchley run), 3.09 (first London marathon and PB time), 3.15 second best marathon time and 3.31 without stopping. Walked at 35km drinks station and got a bottle of energy drink—not sure what was in it, but I did not feel hungry afterwards. The last 8km along the sea front was with a helping breeze and a wonderful view of the ferries coming in and out of Oostende against the blue sky in the distance. I ran with a Belgium for about 5km but unusually no talking and then at 41km I met my wonderful daughter Astrid who ran the last km with me. Soon we were in the car on the way back to Antwerp for a nice cup of tea and a hot bath. I was pleased to get Jacques his fourth Belgian marathon medal. Astrid was pleased with her half marathon time of 1hr 48min. She was to run 1hr 44min in Cyprus a year later.

That evening we went to the nearby town of Leir and had an excellent Chinese meal and then a few beers in his local billiards bar. We were in bed by 3am. We treated Jacques to a horse and coach ride around Antwerp on Sunday morning and then caught the 5pm Euro-Star train via Brussels to London not forgetting the Belgian Chocolates for my long suffering wife.

37M THE 25TH EURO-ASIAN MARATHON – ISTANBUL 2003

Turkish delight and fireworks

This was to be my first time in Asia – only a mile into Asia but still in Asia.

The marathon start overlooked the famous British built bridge that crossed the Bhosphorous linking Europe with Asia. We looked down on the bridge and Europe ahead. This time my then 17-year-old daughter Astrid joined me on the trip. She had entered for the 15 km race. She would be running the first 10km with me, which was great for both of us. I was now at a different school, The Coopers and Coburn School in East London and was running for their elected charity – St Francis Hospice.

ISTANBUL ARMED GUARD AT START OF MARATHON

Security was tight due to problems with the Kurdish minority but we were free to wander around the city. We stayed in Taksim in the newer part of the city and after some difficulty managed to find the place for the marathon registration. On arriving in our hotel, there was an electric power failure just as we entered the lift and had to carry our luggage up three flights of stairs. This power failure was one of many we had to endure during our stay in Istanbul. We then found an Italian type restaurant and managed to carbohydrate load-up for an early start the next day. We were bused several kilometres to the start across the Bhosphorous Bridge, protected by soldiers with Kalashnikovs, which to say the least was a bit scary. It was a clear cool day – great for running. At the race start we put our spare kit on the buses and were watched and guarded by several soldiers as we did so. There were a few thousand runners present, the majority of them were running in the 15km. Some of the Muslim women runners were wearing hijabs.

The start turned out to be very unusual. There was a count down and just on the zero and only metres from me there was a large explosion with flashing lights all over the place. I thought we were dead! No, we were still alive – it was the Turkish way of starting the marathon. It was an extraordinary way of starting due to the fact that there had been several explosions previously in the city. A week or so after we left Istanbul, the British Embassy was blown up along with a synagogue killing several people.

We streamed across the Bosporus Bridge, well guarded, back into Europe. The streets were wide and not too crowded with runners. I noticed a few of the younger local runners wanting to have a chat with my daughter but she did not drop her pace. We parted company near the old city with a clear view of the Blue Mosque and my daughter made her way back to finish in the Besiktas football stadium.

ISTANBUL WITH DAUGHTER (IN 15KM RACE) TEA PLEASE BLUE MOSQUE IN BACKGROUND

One runner, a local lad, caught my eye. He had no running number, wore blue jeans and ran in a pair of leather shoes with flapping loose soles that made a very loud clattering noise. I was impressed with his exuberance and his ability to run with us for about ten miles before he gave up. We carried out along the coast west towards the airport before turning to come back along the same road. At this point, the Blue Mosque was but a mere spec on the horizon. It was a long trek back and some time before the Blue Mosque became more clearly defined. I noticed scores of tall blocks of flats lining the horizon for miles. They reminded me of some of the 3000 blocks of flats over 25 stories high that make up Shanghai, which has a population similar to that of Istanbul's 17 million inhabitants. The last 10 km was hard going as is usual in any marathon, but made even harder by the lack of water drink stations. Getting to the Blue Mosque gave me the extra impetus to push on the last few km to the Besiktas football stadium. I was very surprised to find that the stadium was almost full with some thirty thousand spectators—all young men who had clearly found something to do on a Sunday afternoon. I managed to finish with my usual sprint, which got a cheer, to the finish in just under 4 hours.

In the evening after the marathon we decided to go to an Irish Pub to celebrate with a beer or six. After some searching we found The James Joyce Bar and on entering were presented with a laminated notice informing us that the pub had no Irish beer or spirits due to Turkish import restrictions but could provide some Turkish equivalents. An Irish Pub with no Irish beer was a first for me. Surprisingly, the Turkish beer turned out to be fairly palatable and we were pleased to find the bar had an excellent couple of resident musicians from the west of Ireland, We were served by a beautiful dark haired brown eyed Kerry girl who was married to an equally dark haired brown eyed Turkish co-owner. In this case it seems that like attracts like. Just as we had our drinks to hand the lights went out and the candles were lit which gave the place a friendly romantic west of Ireland feel. The musicians managed to play and sing without electrical backup and it was not long before my daughter was dancing an Irish jig or two in bare feet on the small stage, her performance being enhanced by the flickering candlelights. I always told her that her years of Irish dancing classes would come in useful. As midnight approached, some Norwegian oilman came in and this gave my daughter a chance to further excel, this time using her fluent Norwegian. I also noticed that we seemed to have more women present who sat in pairs in the various nooks and crannies of the bar. The ladies of the night had arrived and I do not think that they come to do some belly dancing or an Irish jig, well at least not in the pub. It was time for my daughter and I to leave.

The next morning we had time to explore some of old Istanbul and the Blue Mosque was our main priority. Impressive from the outside and with some very elaborate blue tiling inside, it was essentially a large domed empty space. Maybe it was designed to reflect the previous desert tent existence of many in the Arab world. For me it lacked the sculpture, imagery and artistic creativity of say St Peters, but as Islam does not allow human imagery, it restricts opportunity for elaborated artistic expression of human joy and suffering. The old Bazaar was the usual hive of activity with a large range of exotic spices and Persian carpets and much else.

We took a taxi drive and 'raced' back to the airport. Our driver wore no seat belt, chain smoked, did some sort of continuous football speak whilst looking directly at me and my daughter in the back seat and was very disappointed when I did not accept on of his proffered cigarettes.

As we waited for our plane my daughter saw the opportunity to do some 'duty free' shopping, the outcome was that she just had to have the most gorgeous pair of Gucci sunglasses and after a credit card payment of £120, they were hidden in the deepest recesses of her travel bag. Still I think I got off lightly, she might have wanted a Gucci travel bag. Daughters sometimes get there way with dads, even if my none too pleased wife had to make do with a box of Turkish delights.

Still a girl who can do an Irish jig in bare feet in candle light in an Irish Bar with no Irish beer and talk fluently in Norwegian to oilmen deserves something special now and then.

THE REAL RUNNER'S MARATHONS

A few hundred runners on country roads or empty industrial suburbs observed by the few dog walkers and where the bleating of Sheep can be as motivating as the roar of the big city crowds.

2M HARLOW MARATHON OCT 1984

The Milk Run

I decided to do this marathon only four weeks before the race start. I still had a residual of fitness left over from my London marathon earlier in the year. I would not be able to build up a lot of stamina to cope well with hitting the wall over the last six miles—proper marathon training takes time in months as well as mileage training if one wants to get a time close to 3 hours.

A work colleague had told me about the Harlow marathon. He had been a former mayor of the town and in 1984 was still a town councillor so he was keen that I should run this marathon, especially after my London marathon success and the fact that my wife was Norwegian. Harlow was designed and built as a new town—close to the small historic old Harlow—to accommodate people from overcrowded and poor accommodation in London. Surprisingly as an inland town, it was twinned with the seaport of Stavanger in Norway. As town councilor he was able to enjoy many a trip to Stavanger and the nearby fjords and had sampled Norwegian Gravlaks long before it became a popular world salmon dish. I never did find out what the Norwegians thought of their inland twin new town; but I do know that my colleague supplied them with quantities of the excellent locally distilled Gilbey's Gin which must have gone down well as Stavanger was situated close to the Norwegian ' bible belt' where alcohol consumption was very much frowned upon.

The course was a figure of eight with the start and finish at the stadium situated at the centre of the eight. The weather was dry, dull and cool which were ideal marathon conditions. There were only about 1000 runners and I was able to keep up with a small group of 3hour pace men until about four miles from the finish when I began to feel tired and hungry. There were no isotonic drinks or energy snacks in those days, just the odd cup of water every few miles. The new town had long avenues that seemed even longer towards the finish. I was not aware of carbohydrate energy loading prior to a marathon back in 1984. The last mile was a real struggle; even going around the racetrack for the last 400 yards was difficult. My finishing time of 3hr 15 min was to be my second best ever for the marathon. The marathon was sponsored by Unigate Milk and a few free cartons of milk put some life back into me, it tasted even better because it was many years since I had my last free milk as a school boy in London which alas was stopped in the 1970s. There was also the bonus of only a quick 15-minute drive home to a long hot bath. Even after the bath, I needed to have a few hours in bed to recover from my exertions.

On Monday morning, I placed my medal on my Harlow colleague's desk – he did not believe I would do the marathon. He was soon over in my office to congratulate me; his town's honour had been saved.

17M ABINGDON, OXFORDSHIRE MARATHON 1994

Starting last and enjoying it

It is extraordinary that the only two marathons that I was the last runner to start should be within two weeks of each other in 1994: New York and Abingdon. I was last to start in New York because I fell asleep in the preparation area and at Abingdon because the boom in car boot sales and associated traffic jams delayed me in my 60 mile drive from Hertford. I suppose it is not so surprising that England has taken to car boot sales and Sunday shopping, after all was it not Napoleon that referred to England as a nation of shopkeepers.

There was also a link between this marathon and the Cherbourg marathon—celebrating the 50th Anniversary of the D-day landings in Normandy—that I ran a few weeks earlier. The Abingdon marathon started and finished on an airfield that was a base for bomber and fighter aircraft in the D-day invasion.

Abingdon is a small market town in Oxfordshire and it was very surprising that they were able to organise a marathon with less than 1000 runners; but sponsorship from the local brewery Morland, who brew excellent strong ale called 'Speckled Hen', was helpful to the organisers. I think all marathon runners should run a small local marathon as well as the big city ones in order to experience the loneliness of the long distance runner where most of your motivation has to come from within.

I arrived at the airfield on a beautiful October sunny day and got started twelve minutes after all the other runners and it would have been even later if I had not arrived all kitted up and ready to run. The long run down the empty runway was an unnerving experience but nerves were soon soothed after I passed the first few rural cottages and noticed the residents shouting some real encouragement. I now could empathise with those marathon runners who struggle along behind the main field but I have to say that I quite enjoyed the sympathy of the few spectators for the less fortunate. It was not long before I got some real pace into my running and soon caught up with my fellow tail end runners. After an hour, I had reached the main pack of runners and my spirits soared when I caught up with a man running his 100th marathon, more so because he was a few years older than I was. My enthusiasm was a little dashed when I noticed his bandaged knees, calf supports and his strange running gait as if he was trying to get to the nearest accident and emergency hospital unit. I was not sure at all that I would want to run 100 marathons and join the 100-marathon club if I ended up looking like this chap. I have never set a target of running a fixed number of marathons, as I have always believed that running is for life, health and enjoyment. I am happy to run two or three marathons a year with a variety of venues and countries. I want to be able to run not walk my marathons in decent times. I do admire the efforts of those that do run a great number of marathons. In 2009 I ran the tough Cornish Marathon and met a guy who had already run 350 marathons and had set a target of 500 before the opening of the London Olympics in 2012 which effectively means running 50 marathons a year. Bearing in mind how few marathons there are in the winter and in high summer, that he could suffer sickness and injuries, he has set himself a very difficult task. Still as he has already run 350 he must know what he is doing in setting such a goal.

The run through the rural English countryside and its idyllic villages was a great enjoyment and contrasted greatly with city marathons. One felt at one with nature and at peace with the world. The route was along winding country roads and there was always something to catch the eye or ear in what was a lovely tranquil autumnal day. Although I slowed down towards the end, I finished with a clock time of 3hr 41min so just about broke 3hr 30min. I cannot be sure as to the exact time as there were no individual electric time chips in those days.

At the time of writing I was surprised to find that the Abingdon marathon is still going strong and is in fact oversubscribed for the 1000 entry limit but it no longer starts on the airfield which is alas no more.

45M 31ST DUCHY OF CORNWALL MARATHON MARCH 2007

Running on water only.

For the spring term in 2007 I managed to secure a very pleasant part-time teaching contract back again at one of my all-time favourite schools – The City of London School for Girls. The school is set in the heart of the Barbican in the city of London and one has all the facilities of the city on your doorstep. The school uses the splendid Guild Hall for its prize giving and orchestral performances and is under the governance of The Corporation of the City of London. I like the school most because of the wonderful girls that attend. They may be very bright and talented but they respond to teachers with personality and purpose in their teaching programme. Their sense of enquiry and open mindedness is a pleasure to experience as a teacher.

For the year 2007, the school's elected charity was 'The Tuberous Sclerosis Association.' As I was only there for a term, I had to find a marathon that would give me time to give assemblies to support sponsorship and leave enough time to collect in the sponsorship money before the end of term. As luck would have it, there was the AAA Cornwall marathon in early March. The first Duchy of Cornwall marathon took place in 1977 when there were only 13 UK marathons listed in The Road Runners' Club Handbook and the 'Duchy' was ranked equal toughest with the Isle of Wight marathon. Five years latter, and due to 'marathon mania' sparked by the first London marathon, there were nearly 150 marathons listed including the Snowdonia marathon in Wales that now took the title of the toughest UK marathon.

The Cornwall marathon became a favourite for the more serious club runner and was run from Land's End along the north coast to the mining town of Redruth. Recently the course was changed to include two laps starting and finishing in Redruth and includes a climb up to a coastal stretch, followed by another climb inland back up to Redruth. It is still a tough course, especially when running against a stiff Atlantic southwesterly coastal breeze on the cliff tops.

For some time I have been worried about my carbon footprint when using airlines to get to marathon destinations – 34 of my marathons have involved flying, although on several occasions I have taken the opportunity to visit relatives and friends or have a family holiday. Canada, Sweden, Norway, USA, Chile, Iceland, Germany, Ireland and Belgium have fallen into the latter category. This time, and again with only the weekend available, I thought that I would let the train take the strain instead of the plane. This would impress the girls with my green credentials. I discovered that there was no direct train from London to Redruth and the journey would take 9 hours. The journey time and cost turned out to be prohibitive compared to a Ryanair flight to Newquay for 1p return plus taxes, car hire to Redruth costing £40 .Compare that to the £250 for the train and the extra time involved – no contest. It is sad to reflect that the country that invented the railway system should now have one of the most expensive and antiquated rail systems in Europe.

On arriving in Redruth, I was struck how depressed this once proud Cornish mining town was. I asked at the hotel reception if there were any Italian restaurants that I could go to for a bit of pasta hydrocarbon loading and was informed that the last one in the town closed down over a year ago. Luckily, the hotel had a good evening menu and I enjoyed a magnificent crab fish soup almost as good as the one my Norwegian brother-in-law makes. I also had the added pleasure of meeting the hotel manageress in the restaurant who turned out to be a past pupil of mine at Ashlyns School in Berkhamsted. I had taught her GCSE mathematics that she passed with flying colours.

Race day was one of glorious spring sunshine, windy and a pleasant temperature of about 14C. There were only about 300+ race competitors—most of them club runners. The course was a two-lap affair—not my favourite set-up, with the first few kilometres in the town. I could not help noticing the large number of Methodist chapels, many of them dilapidated. The Methodist influence is great in the mining areas of Cornwall and Wales. As we headed out of town to the north coast of Cornwall in an anti-clockwise direction, we encountered a long inclined hill with a stiff coastal breeze to content with, but a great view to compensate. I managed to get a drink of water at the first of the few water stations along the way; but noticed that there were many named labelled bottles on the table. Unknowns to me, runners had to provide their own isotonic drinks, so for me it was back to the tough old days of the 1980s—water only. As the race was The Cornish AAA Championship, runners were able to order special drinks before the race – a luxury unknown to me. After about 16km we turned inland and encountered another long uphill climb back up to Redruth. As I completed the first lap I realised that I would have to face two big hill climbs again but this time at 30km and 36km not to mention the stiff coastal breeze. I managed the first hill ok but the second was a real struggle and I had to walk some of the way up. I surprised myself with a strong 2km finish in the town to just break the 4-hour barrier. Despite the hills, I found the run a very stimulating challenge, but was glad not to have to run it on a rain swept windy Cornish day that is often the norm in these parts.

The race started and finished in my hotel grounds, so it was one of the earliest baths for me after the race. At the presentation ceremony in the hotel, I was surprised to find that I got third place in my age category and my first ever road racing trophy in over 25 years of running marathons.

On the car journey back to Newquay airport I took the coastal route to enjoy the fine scenery of the north Cornish coast—this time letting the car take the strain. I was able to give a race report on the school's website in time for Monday morning assembly and was very pleases with the sponsorship that the girls and staff of The City of London Girls' School gave me.

FROM BARCELONA TO LISBON

30 M MARATO DE BARCELONA MARCH 2000

ON THE RAMBLA BARCELONA 2000 30ᵀᴴ MARATHON

Viva La Catalunya

It took along time to get round to doing a marathon in Spain. As Barcelona was the venue for the 1992 Olympics it seemed to be the most ideal city for a marathon. It was strange that they did not use the Olympic stadium as a starting or finishing point for the race, but instead we had the start some 30km up the coast north of the city with the finish in a big exhibition centre about two kilometers from the centre.

I had difficulty trying to book a hotel and ended up having to stay the Saturday night in a run down hotel near a local railway station and the Sunday night in a luxury 5 star hotel on the famous Las Ramblas in the heart of the city. The later was booked courtesy of an internet company called 'lastminute.com' but still cost £100 a night without breakfast. My room was called 'The Rab Butler Suite', after the Hollywood actor Clark Gable who starred in 'Gone with the Wind'.

On the bus on the way in from the airport, I sat opposite a beautiful blond blue eyed girl – not quite what you expect in Spain. There was a chemistry between us that just led me to talk to her. Her English was poor but I worked out that she had just dropped her boy friend off at the airport knew all about Irish dancing and wanted to visit Ireland. This was the first Russian girl that I had ever met but I resisted the temptation to go to a local coffee bar with her for a further chat; but she did have the most amazing blue eyes.

The evening before the marathon I managed to find a small Italian family restaurant in the old city quarter and had my usual pasta with the minestrone soup as a starter. I always judge Italian restaurants by the quality of their minestrone soup and this one had nice fresh vegetables in it and was very tasty.

It was a very early rise – 5.30 am – on race day with no breakfast available. I shared a taxi to the main railway station with a professional veteran marathon runner from the north of Italy. His small wiry muscular frame suggested that he was capable of a good time and from his attire, I deduced that he was sponsored by the carmaker Fiat. His English and my Italian were non existent so we had to make do with some hand signals and facial gestures – oh how I regret not having had the opportunity to learn more foreign languages at school and later in life. We took a double-decked train up the coast to the start with pleasant views of the sea and through sleepy small towns all enlivened by a clear blue sky unspoilt by airplane contrails that we get nowadays.

Conditions for running were ideal and so it was running vest and shorts for me and after an extra dab of Vaseline on my vital parts we were on our way. There were only a few thousand runners in the race and it was not long before I was running at my race pace around the wide streets of the local town and then heading south. Over half the marathon involved a run down the coast through seaside villages along a very serene sea on our left. I could see Barcelona city in the distance and the spires of Gaudi's Sagrada Familia cathedral; but for several kilometers, they did not appear to get any nearer. I had a similar experience running along the Bosporus back into Istanbul when the Blue Mosque seemed to remain small and in the distance. There was little banter between the runners and that included the Spanish but we did get the odd 'Ole' or two from the early morning coffee drinkers in local cafes.

It got a bit more atmospheric as we entered central Barcelona and ran up and down the Las Ramblas, a distance of 2.5 kilometers. This was the high point for spectator support. Rambla means to walk in Spanish. I had already run over 35km so there was a temptation to do just that; but I could not let down the spectators and managed to keep running the last few kilometers through endless blocks of residential flats to finish in a very pleasing time of 3hr 36 min at the age of 54 years.

Early Sunday evening after a nice long relaxing bath in my 5 star hotel back on the Las Ramblas I decided to try out a the local fish dish. With my poor Spanish I ended up with a baked fish dish that was very dry – what I would have done for a decent fish sauce or a pan-fried fish. I did have a nice bottle of dry white wine that I did not finish; but it did not go to waste. I gave the remaining contents to a very grateful Scottish couple. Later in one of the Irish pubs nearby I met a very nice Irish barmaid who was not happy about how her Catalan boss was treating her. I ended up in an argument with the boss, fuelled now by a few drinks and the white wine I had earlier. He was on the point of ordering me out when in came some Manchester United supporters, in Spain for a European cup match against Valencia, who with a bit of help from me came to my support; the boss knew he was outnumbered and retreated. As for the rest of the evening I can only remember being carried by a group of blue suited Catalan Club members up the Las Ramble as I shouted Viva La Republica Cataluña. To think that earlier in the day I was running up and down the Las Ramblas and now I was being carried.

The next day I got up late and was too late for breakfast. However, I did notice the magnificence of my Rab Butler suite but sadly I was in no state to appreciate its opulence and décor. I went back to the Las Ramblas for a brunch but this time I was less elated than I was twelve hours earlier and spent my last couple of hours in the nearby medieval cathedral in a very repentant mood.

On the bus on the way back to the airport I thought of the Russian blue eyed blond but now I was glad to be in my own company and on the way home to my own blue eyed blond wife.

Viva La Cataluña.

32M MARATONA CIDADE DE LISBOA 25TH NOV 2000

Rosa Mota's last marathon

For late November it was still quite mild but very wet. It was the usual Friday evening get away from Heathrow to be back late Sunday evening. Unfortunately, I was carrying an Achilles tendon injury picked up in having to run on very soft wet ground in one of the wettest autumns in years. It was a reoccurrence of the same problem that I had in May in the Copenhagen marathon. The school that I then taught at was Mill Hill in London and they have two wonderful cross-country courses. One of the courses goes through a valley with a large cricket ground and it was here that I stretched my tendons a little too much in the boggy ground. I was also running with a female colleague who was a very good middle distance runner and I needed to keep up with her – male pride and all that.

On arriving in Lisbon, I was quite surprised how hilly the city was; but fortunately, the marathon course was run in the main along the main riverbank and so was quite flat. It was a two-lap course and possible the most boring that I have ever ran. It started in the city centre and then went out along the river and back to the centre. This was repeated for a second time. The marathon was to be the last for Rosa Moto a great Portuguese runner and London marathon winner.

For the first half of the marathon I managed to keep going with a reduced stride so as not to over stretch my Achilles tendon. The second out and back was more problematic and I had to walk after 25km; but managed to adopt a run—walk—run routine. I have never counted so many telegraph poles in my life before. At first, I ran three pole spaces and walked one. I then got down to running one space and walking the next. Time went very slowly and the distance covered seemed to get longer and longer. There was very little crown support So I was relying entirely on my own motivation; even more so in the second half of the race because most of the entries were for the half marathon. I finished with a time of 4hr 5min and this was my second marathon in succession over 4 hours. The message here is look after your Achilles tendons.

After the marathon I had some time before my evening flight and took the opportunity to buy some vintage port to have with Stilton cheese at Christmas. I was nearly tempted to open a bottle of port when I got to the airport and discovered that there was a 24-hour strike by airport staff and that I was not able to depart until 6am. It was not all bad news as I met up with a nice Brazilian man who was heading home after a two-year stay in London where he worked in the leather business. We discussed the environmental and population issues faced by South America. One fact remained in my mind when he told me that when staying in Mexico city he had to queue up to get into an over crowded cinema for a 10 am showing on a Monday morning!. How long was the queue to get in on a Friday evening I wondered?

Leaving Lisbon at 6 am meant I would have to go straight to school. Would I arrive in time for my first lesson at 9am? Thankfully, my wife, on her way to her work in north London dropped off my work suit and fresh underwear at my school. After a long tube ride from Heathrow airport followed by a taxi ride to the school, I arrived for my A' Level Mathematics lesson only 15 minutes late.

It was raining again.

"Train don't strain"

Anon

SCANDINAVIA—CELTIC RAID ON THE VIKING CAPITALS

19M HELSINKI MARATHON JULY 1995

The Flying Finns

One of the strongest and widely used words in Finnish is 'sisu', which means **guts.** For marathon running, you certainly need a lot of sisu. Finland has a long tradition of long distance running. Their most outstanding runner was Paavo Nurmi, winner of nine Olympic gold medals. Another great Finnish runner was Lasse Viren who won the 5km and 10km gold medals at the Montreal Olympics in 1976 and then came 5th in the final event – the marathon. He was also one of the first athletes to go in for blood transfusions to oxygenate the blood, which gave the advantages of training at high altitude without the need to do so. The practice, I believe, is now banned.

By 1952 Nurmi had retired from running but was given the honour of carrying the Olympic Torch in the specially designed stadium to light the Olympic Flame and so open the Helsinki Olympic Games. It was incredible that war torn London was able to host the 1948 Olympics; but it was even more incredible that a country of just over 4 million inhabitants was able to host the 1952 Games. Finland had fought a brave defence against a full scale Russian invasion early on in the Second World War and suffered great loss of life. By 1952, they had just finished paying war reparations to Russia. In honour of Paavo Nurmi there is a wonderful bronze statue of him in full running stride at the entrance to the stadium. The Olympic stadium was to be the venue for the start and finish of the 15th Helsinki City marathon in late July 1995.

For this marathon I went with a Sports Tour Company in a party that included about 20 runners. It was the summer school holidays, so I was able to spend 5 days in Helsinki and make a little holiday of the trip instead of the usual mad weekend rush. There are very few marathons in Europe in July, but Finland is well to the North and is not too hot or so I thought. Well, I was wrong and for my duration we had maximum daily temperatures of 25 C plus. The organisers were aware that it can be very warm at this time of year and arranged for a 3pm marathon start. Even so, it turned out to be one of the hottest weather conditions that I experienced.

This marathon also had an extra dimension for me. Besides the pleasure of running in a country with a great tradition of long distance running there was the pressing need to achieve a time of less than 3hr 25min in order to qualify for the 100th Boston Marathon the following year.

Surprisingly there were only about 1000 participants in the race—maybe the many absent Finns were out swimming and fishing in the hundreds of lakes that surround the capital city—a sensible thing to do given the good weather. The course itself was very countrified with plenty of lakeside and seaside running, but there were a few challenging hills. One got the feel of spaciousness, as I found the case to be with all the Scandinavian capitals I have run in. Sadly, for me by the 25km marker I was really feeling the heat and struggling to keep up with my 3h25min pace. At 30km I walked at a drinks station and knew then that I was not going to achieve my target and pure survival became my primary target. With a lot of effort and copious sweating, I finished in 3hr 36min. Nevertheless, despite the heat and my failure to achieve my aim, I had a great experience and well worth the trip.

Helsinki then and now is an expensive city in terms of accommodation, food and drink. When we arrived at our somewhat basic hotel, other members in the group looked towards me for some idea as to where to base ourselves for some entertainment. When the English see an Irishman, they see someone who should know all about partying or the Craic as we Irish call it. I asked the receptionist how many Irish pubs there were in the city. Two she replied – O'Malley's and The Dubliners. Well as my name is O'Reilly it had to be O'Malley's and so off we went and a good evening was had by one and all. There was another Irishman in the group, an hotelier from north London. On the plane I noticed that he was carrying several large boxes of" After Eight' chocolates including one in the shape of a large mantle piece clock. For the two days before the marathon, unusually for me, I minimised my social contacts and after all I had a time target to achieve. I made do with some pleasant walks around the city and its harbour area. After the marathon the first member of the group that I met was my Irishman who by now was carrying fewer boxes of chocolates and clearly had given some away, but to whom? I was soon to find out. We arranged to meet later in the evening and it was a further two days before I met other members of the group who told me they had a great time in O'Malley's and could not understand why I did not join them. I discovered that our Irishman had been very popular with the 'Ladies of the Night—and Day' from nearby Estonia who really liked his After Eights chocolates. He assured me that they had been a great source of comfort for his final marathon preparations and gave me a grand tour of the local clubs. I played the role of the exhausted post marathon tourist drinking copious amounts of herbal tea.

My new found Irish friend and I spent the last morning on a boat trip round the harbour and islands in beautiful sunny weather. As a trained publican, he made sure not to take the first pint of the day served by the boat's barman. Soon we were on the way home and I stopped off at his hotel in London for a farewell pint with him. His wife did not seem too pleased to see him. I suppose running a hotel and bar whilst your husband is away giving chocolates to the girls of Finland and Estonia does not endear one to their love one.

22M STOCKHOLM MARATHON JUNE 1996

The Venice of the North

Stockholm was the venue for the 1912 Olympics and the original brick built stadium is still operational and formed the venue for the finish of the 1996 marathon. There are three other Olympic stadiums that I finished city marathons in: Athens, Helsinki and Munich.

Stockholm in early June is a magical place with long summer evenings, very clear air and a superb quality of light that enhances the many waterways and golden yellow walls of the buildings in the Gamle Staden (Old City). Stockholm is a city that has evolved over 300 years without experiencing the destruction of warfare and its coastal setting with many ships and waterways makes it a 'Venice of the North'.

The marathon course was two laps with several bridges to cross and mostly run in and around the city centre. Unusually, it is held on a Saturday early afternoon, which as it transpired turned out to be very advantageous for me. One of the main reasons for selecting the Stockholm marathon was the opportunity to visit my brother Vincent and his Swedish wife. They met in London in the 1970s and married in my sister-in-law's home and lovely Hansiatic town of Visby, Gotland, in the early 1980s. My brother is a multi-media

Artist. He has designed some very interesting and thought provoking outdoor Art structures in Stockholm and Visby.

The week before the marathon I was on my wife's annual school trip to the German Rhineland and took the opportunity to fly direct to Stockholm from Frankfurt in glorious afternoon sun shine. I can remember having a wonderful view of Copenhagen, a city that I would run a marathon in the year 2000, and of the islands of the Skagerrak. It was so clear that I reckon I might have been able to see with a set of binoculars the little Danish mermaid sitting all alone on her rock.

My nephew Liam from England had already arrived in Stockholm with the intention of running the marathon as well; but injury ruled him out. Nevertheless, he was intent on enjoying the trip, which was greatly aided by the attention of several very nice Swedish girl admirers. He and my brother went with me to register for the marathon and saw the place where Vincent's famous Pyramid art structure was on display. Afterwards we returned to Vincent's flat for a very nice vegetarian meal prepared by his wife Eva. It certainly was not a carbohydrate loading meal, so I would not be carrying any extra weight on my run and the odd pangs of hunger that I had during the race took my mind off the physical pain in the latter stages of the race. Later we went out to see the City lit up by the late evening sun and it was not long before we ended up in a nightclub surrounded by a bevy of beautiful Swedish girls with Liam as the main attraction. I went easy on the beer and not only because of its cost. At about 2.30 am I began to be a little concerned about my bedtime and I left the club only to be greeted by bright early morning sunshine. It was a new day and I still had not been to bed. I would be running a marathon in less than ten hours. A little bit of panic set in and I left the others as they headed for their next nightclub and luckily managed to find my way back to the flat. My shared bedroom had heavy curtains and it was possible to block out the bright early morning sun and create a little bit of night. After I had a few hours sleep I got up and made myself a little breakfast, whilst the others slept. I found some Swedish crisp bread and some light sweet bread. What I would have done for a chunky wholemeal loaf – still it took the edge off my hunger pangs.

I managed to hire an unofficial and rather battered taxi to get me to the stadium and arrived early enough to prepare mentally and physically for the task ahead. The weather was a little cloudy but dry with a temperature about 18 Celsius – good conditions for marathon running. As it was a two lap Marathon, I had time to take in the sights on the way and to count the bridges. The atmosphere from runners and spectators was a little restrained, after all this was Sweden. The roads were wide and smooth and there was plenty of room to run in comfort and get a good marathon time. The crowds were more enthusiastic and animated near the Gamle Staten. For me things got a little more exciting when running up a long slope at 40km I saw my nephew Liam running towards me – recovered from his nightclub exploits—with a can of coke. A fizzy can of coke is the last thing one needs in a marathon, but it is the thought that counts. I then saw my brother shuffling towards me with a very large professional TV camera on his shoulder. No complaints from me, after all it was a chance to be filmed for posterity. With all this unusual attention, I was inspired to run the last 2km in some style to finish in 3hr 43min – a good result for me.

On the way back home, we travelled on the metro and Vincent took more film recordings, not just views looking up my nostrils, but of other passengers from various elevations. I suppose everybody likes a bit of attention and after all Vincent had to do his artist bit. To this day, he continues his artistic work on several fronts but I am still waiting to see the results of his 1996 film recordings. On second thoughts, maybe it should stay in his archives.

27M OSLO MARATHON 9ᵀᴴ SEPT 1998

Round and round we go again

It had taken 14 years since my first marathon to finally get to run in Norway – my wife's country of birth.

Over 1000 years earlier the Norwegian branch of the Vikings had paid a visit and then stayed to found the city of my birth – Dublin. I will not mention the rape and pillage or the famous victory by the Irish King Boru at the battle of Clontaf in 1014 in any detail here. Suffice it to state that it was my turn to take on the Vikings on their home patch.

The race started and finished at the Bislett Stadium. In the past, the stadium was the venue for many world records at middle distance running. I remember being taken to the stadium by my Norwegian uncle to see the great English 1500meter runner David Moorcroft who later became president of the UK AAA. I was astonished by the length of his stride, pace and rhythm of his running.

The marathon course was one of the oddest I have ever run. It comprised 4 laps through the city centre south of the stadium and two laps north of the stadium through the famous or ' infamous' Frogner Park. Most of the runners were entered in the half-marathon with a few hundred running the full marathon or ' Helmarathon' in Norwegian. It did turn out to be a bit of a hellish marathon for me.

I finished work on Friday at 4pm and was in my cousin's house by 11.30pm. I had a couple of beers and then went straight to bed. My cousin has a splendid detached wooden house near the famous Holmenkollen ski jump, built for the 1952 Winter Olympics. As was the case with the Stockholm and Helsinki marathons, this marathon took place on a Saturday afternoon.

The weather was dry, cloudy and cool – great for running. For this marathon I wore my beloved Helle Hanson sweat wicking vest, shorts and my head sweatband. Because of my lack of eyebrows to deflect the sweat, I need the headband in all weathers. From photographs I note that my Nike trainers were having their third and last marathon outing.

The first lap was downhill into the city centre passing the Royal Palace, the Old University of Oslo, the National Theatre, the House of Parliament and around Akerhus Fortress. The later was the focus for some military action against the invading German army in 1940. In admiring all these famous landmarks I noticed another very popular one – an Irish Pub. This gained a greater significance for me as the marathon progressed.

We then made our way back uphill past the stadium and into the Frogner Park. This park is world famous for its nude granite statues – 600 of them. Some of the nudes are chiselled out of a block of granite 14 meters high and one structure was a tower of 121 figures in all with adult nudes at the bottom, spiralling upwards to children at the top. The sculptor Gustav Vigeland saw it as a struggle for existence. I was soon to learn exactly what he meant.

On the second lap through the city, I now noticed that there were scores of people inside and outside the Irish Pub with glasses holding a black liquid with a white top. I ran past at a brisk pace. As we again ran uphill towards the stadium, most of the runners peeled away towards the half-marathon finish. The few hundred marathon runners left headed back to the Frogner Park. This time I had more time to contemplate the meaning of the tower of interwoven stone figurines. I was beginning now to slow down and seize up a bit. I was glad that loop would be my last time in this park, otherwise I might stop and inadvertently form a static union with one of the statues—hopefully faith would have co-joined me to one of the muscular busty young ladies. However, I still had to face another big challenge.

We ran down hill again for a third lap of the city centre. Just past the Opera House I had a great surprise. To my amazement I saw my brother-in-law and his son waving and calling my name. They had come unknown to me to see me run from their home town of Hamar some 80 miles north of Oslo. Back up the hill and again down for the last lap of the city centre. This time the only landmark that I had in mind was that Irish Pub. My thirst was now reaching a crescendo. Pub or no pub I always get extra thirsty towards the end of a marathon even after taking in a lot of water early on in the race. I do not know how I got the willpower to run past the pub for the fourth time. The place was now heaving and supported by Irish folk music. I made a resolution there and then – I would come back that evening.

I managed to finish in a time of 3hr 42min, which was quite pleasing.

That evening we returned to the pub and left in a bit of a blur at 3am. I even managed to talk my way to the front of a very long taxi queue—it helps to show your marathon medal – pick my two colleagues off the pavement and get them home to their wives. They certainly appreciated my efforts the next morning!

So Tusen Takk, Ja vi elsker Norge—A thousand thanks, Norway we love you.

31M COPENHAGEN MARATHON MAY 2000

Wonderful, Wonderful, Copenhagen but where's the Mermaid.

For me my run in Copenhagen was far from wonderful. One of my Achilles tendons was playing up and I could get very few longish runs done in the weeks leading up to this marathon. I found the second half of the race hard going through near empty long streets. I had to resort to my run walk run strategy to get to the finish. My finishing time was my slowest in my marathon career to date and my first over 4 hours.

I arrived mid Saturday in perfect calm sunny weather, yet our pilot still managed to overshoot the runway and had to have a second go at landing the plane. I would be taking the Sunday evening flight back to London for work as usual on Monday morning. My family and I had visited Copenhagen once before when we failed to find the little Mermaid. As of 2010 I still have not yet seen the little Mermaid. I think she only exists in the tales of Hans Christian Anderson. However we do have one very vivid and real memory of our last visit to Denmark.

Whilst camping near the Danish western coast in wild countryside with a few derelict farmhouses we were buzzed by NATO military jets screaming only a few hundred feet over our bright blue tent at 6.00 am in the morning. A few minutes later, we were surrounded by military police. In the early morning light I could see the large tracks of tanks from previous military exercises and now we could hear the rumble of the tanks getting closer. They had us out of there in minutes and this despite my wife's plea in good Danish to have breakfast first. Even I did not fancy tank scrambled eggs. No, it was not a good idea to pitch tent in the path of a full scale military exercise.

I was actually pleased to see that Copenhagen was virtually devoid of people and traffic on marathon weekend. This was certainly not the case mid-week when London's Arsenal fans were in the city for a European Championship game. They left not so many tank trails behind them more a trail of broken windows, bottles and telephone kiosks. Maybe they should have been transferred to western Denmark for a dawn military exercise. I can only say that the Danes have long since lost their Viking ways and are perhaps much too tolerant towards their riotous visitors.

One bright note to this trip occurred when I managed to get a £100 suite in The Palace Hotel right opposite The Tivoli in the city's main square courtesy of lastminute.com. I had the Greta Gabor suite with a very nice marathon breakfast included. I found a good Italian restaurant by the historic Nye Haven canal with all the garlic bread that I could eat.

After the race I found myself an Irish Pub and got talking to the two young and very friendly Gay Irish proprietors. They were impressed by my knowledge of the qualities of Nigerian Guinness and after six free pints of the black stuff I was ready to head out to the airport but not before I presented them with one of my spare marathon medals. A friend of mine visited the pub a couple of years later and the two lads were still there and the medal was in pride of place over the bar. I forgot to ask them if they knew where that little mermaid was but then they were probably not very interested in mermaids.

ICELAND COD WARS AND BANK WARS

38M REYKJAVIK MARATHON 21 AUGUST 2004 ICELAND

A surprise for my wife

It is normally too hot to run marathons in Europe in August, but in Iceland it is an ideal month for a marathon. My wife had always wanted to go to Iceland. As a schoolgirl in Norway she had learnt about the Icelandic Sagas and the first Norwegian settlers – many of them exiled from Norway—to inhabit Iceland. The Icelandic long parliament and its unique brand of democracy also caught her imagination. So she was very pleased when I surprised her by an invitation to Iceland. She would not have to wait as she expected to retire before visiting the country. We would spend a week touring the country and then I would run the marathon at the weekend.

The marathon course was very scenic and run on coastal footpaths and in parks within the capital. One nearly always had a view of the sea and surrounding volcanic mountains. The weather was ideal if a little on the hot side—sunny with a slight breeze and about 21C. My training for this marathon was relaxed and it was eleven months since my last marathon in Istanbul. At 58 years old, I had to get used to the physical and mental demands to get another sub 4-hour marathon time. I found it difficult to get in any real long runs in preparation. I did have some unusual 45 minute runs at 35C on holiday in Seville in Spain in July, which meant that running in the heat would not be too big a problem for me. By now, I was cross training more often and my basic training session consisted of a four-mile run on grass paths, followed by a gym session on the rowing machine, bike and cross-trainer. I liked to finish my gym session with a 200 meter plus swim. Nearer the marathon, I increased the bike work and put in a few longer runs. Two weeks before the marathon I put in five consecutive days of 4, 7,5,5 and 4 mile runs for a total weekly of 25 miles. I find this patter of mileage builds up my stamina with little risk of injury.

There were only a few hundred runners in the race with quite a few Canadians running for a charity supporting victims of diabetes. I had a chat with two women from Nottingham, England who had run the 1982 and 1983 London marathons. My first marathon was the 1984 London. They were both sub 4 hour runners but one of them had a stomach problem from the night before coupled to an extraordinary running style. She ran very knock-kneed with her feet kicking outwards as if she was doing a swimming breaststroke. Still she achieved her target despite her ailments. That is what marathon running is all about.

My wife got her first sight of me at the 37 km marker along an open coastal path under a clear blue sky with no other runners in sight. She must have thought that I was out for just a pleasant jog, which it was in a way. Reality caught up with me at 39km when I walked for the first time at a drinks station, but I got going again to finish with a bit of a sprint – at least to me it was—in a time of 3hr 54min. For once, I did not feel too thirsty at the finish and was able to walk the kilometre or so back to our hotel for a shower. I was not too impressed with Icelandic hotel facilities. What I would have paid and done for a nice soak in a bath.

They say that Iceland had forests when the Norwegians first arrived. I did see a few newly planted trees in and around some of the towns but the country is essentially a set of extinct volcanoes sitting on the north Atlantic fault line. There are some benefits in the form of hot geezers and thermal baths. I found swimming in the Blue Lagoon a very uplifting experience – the water is quite dense if a little smelly. In the main Reykjavik swimming baths, one had a choice of pools at 20, 30 or 40C. I could have done with one of these after the marathon. We took a hired car and drove around the south of Iceland. We stayed in a small town close to a large snow clad volcano which had the potential to erupt so it was a somewhat eyrie experience sleeping or trying to sleep in a hotel perched on the edge of this volcano. The following morning I could not resist a swim in my birthday suit in the sea along an empty beech made up of jet-black volcanic sand.

There was a big cultural event in the city on the night of the marathon and is was by far the largest social event in Iceland. I guess about half of the total population of 350,000 was present. We started the evening with a fish dinner at one of the main hotels. It had taken us a week to get a decent fish dish and we greatly enjoyed the fish soup followed by a very tasty monkfish dish. It may be one of the ugliest fish in the sea but it is one of the tastiest when cooked properly. Iceland exports most of its fish and we even saw three Japanese tuna fish trawlers in the harbour who paid for licences to fish in Icelandic waters and so avoided a 'tuna' war unlike the earlier 'cod war' with the UK. Whilst having an after dinner coffee two Icelandic men in their late 20s came in and signalled that they wanted two coffees. They were each talking on their mobile phones. They never spoke a word to each other throughout their stay. They hand signalled that they wanted to pay and left the restaurant still talking on their mobiles. During the street celebrations, I would say that at any one time more than half the people were on their mobile phones. It seems amazing that in such a compact small city so many people felt the need to use their mobile phones. We continued our evening with my now customary visit to an Irish pub. I ordered my first pint of Guinness in a week and after some time, was handed by the bar woman a glass of milk costing £6, well it looked like a glass of milk. As it settled, I had the equivalent of half a pint of Guinness that would have cost me £12 a pint. I went back to the bar and showed the woman how to pour a proper pint of Guinness and in doing so reduced the bar's profits by 50%.

We got talking to an Icelandic couple – I say talking—the man was on and off his mobile for the two hours that we were together. Even my wife and I were asked to talk on his mobile to various relatives and friends, some of them were only about 10 meters away on the other side of the bar. Later, whilst a little more inebriated and on hearing that my wife was Norwegian he launched into a tirade against the Norwegians for the exile and persecution of his ancestors. This may have been 1000 years ago, but to him it was like yesterday. He was particularly bitter about the methods used by Norway to exile and then exploit some of their chieftains to Iceland. He seemed to be somewhat oblivious to the fact that most Icelanders were directly descended from Norwegian stock and their language was related to Old Norse. He also made the claim that about 25% of the Icelandic gene pool was from Irish monastic monks and of which he was very proud. Well I know the Vikings did kidnap a few Irish redheads on their travels to Ireland and the Irish monks did get around a bit—did not St Brendan even get to America describing a place of fire, firmament, smoke and huge chunks of ice on the way?. However, I did not think that they left such a big genetic footprint in Iceland. Mind you, the celibacy of monks was not a big issue over 1000 years ago as it is today. That night in the pub there was plenty of fire, firmament and volcanic eruptions, but my wife coped well with her new role as a representative of imperial oppressors.

At midnight there was a splendid firework display and afterwards we went to a hotel for a final nightcap. The clientele seemed to include most of the top politicians in the country. One well suited man on hearing that my wife and I were from Norway and Ireland came over and sat down right in front of us . He remained there for about 10 minutes just looking at us without uttering a single word. This was a little unnerving but after all this was their big night. I wonder what this man did on the other 364 nights of the year?

The next day the temperature reached an incredible 27C – almost a record for Iceland. We decided to go pony riding on those famous Icelandic ponies and found a riding school about 20km from Reykjavik. The stables was not busy and a pleasant young girl fixed us up with two lively ponies – my wife wanted the most docile one—and then led us on a pony trek across some very rocky landscape and through a river valley with the ponies wading across the river. We were thankful that the ponies seemed to know what to do because we were too busy just trying to stay in the saddle. Icelandic ponies have a repertoire of seven different trots and with my bareback workhorse riding experience as a boy in Ireland; I thought I would try my pony on a gallop. Staying on a galloping pony across the rocky Icelandic landscape is an experience I do not want to repeat.

On the way back, at a steady trot, I said to my wife 'I bet you are glad that you did not wait until you retired to endure this bone shaking experience'.

CANADIAN MAPLELEAFS

29M CANADIAN INTERNATIONAL MARATHON TORONTO OCT 1999

Land of the Kanukes, Moose, Mounties and my sister.

My Canada based sister had already been down to the US to support me in my running of the 97th and 100th Boston marathons so it was high time that I returned the compliment and ran a marathon in Canada.

The early evening flight from London with the gain in time when going west left even more time for another drinking session to add to the first session I had on the flight. My sister and her daughter joined me in a tour. Events caught up with me when I got back to their house. I had a bed for the night in the nicely furnished cellar. A few hours later, I woke up desperate for a wee. Jet lagged and still under the influence, I could not find the light switch in the inky black darkness. I was disorientated and after several minutes feeling my way around endless walls I just could not find my way out of the cellar. There was only one solution and to my utter relief I used a wall as my urinal. The next morning I was involved in a cleaning up operation hoping that my sister would not come down into the cellar. Later that day I decided to have a bath after a 'recovery run' for the marathon the next day. The bathroom was tiled and there was a tile with a handle on it to enable one to get out of the bath and upon levering myself up holding this tile, the tile and half the other tiles came off the wall and into the bath. I managed to stick them back on using some soap and was terrified of telling my sister in case she would worry too much. Instead, I hinted that there was some dampness under the tiles in the bathroom – which there was—and that it would be a good idea to check out with her household insurance if she could get them replaced. A few weeks later, her friend was having a bath and guess what happened – the tiles came off the wall again. Her friend was mortified but my sister remembered what I told her about household insurance and managed to claim for a newly retiled bath. I have since owed up to both incidents and we can laugh about it now—I think!

Compared to the damage I was doing to my sister's house the marathon provided few problems for me and my time of 3hr 32 min was the fastest of my five marathons in North and South America. The October weather was cool and dry and the course had very wide even roads to run on with long highways, some parkland routes and finished in the city centre. Toronto has one of the longest city streets in the world called Yong Street and we ran about 12km of it in a straight line of course. Canadians often comment on how many good grand prix drivers come from Britain and rightly put it down to our winding country roads. Surprisingly the course did not include any runs along Lake Ontario. I was pleased to have the support of my niece along several parts of the course and the chance to talk to a few of the other runners to help break the tedium of those long stretches of highway.

A high point of any trip to Toronto is the opportunity to visit their wonderful outdoor museum depicting the settler developments since the formation of Canada and not forgetting a trip up the CN Tower that was once the tallest man made structure in the world.

34M 2ND CANADIAN MARATHON—NIAGARA FALLS INTERNATIONAL PEACE MARATHON OCT 2001

NIAGAR FALLS MARATHON AT START WITH SISTER AND NEW YORK RUNNER (NO991) 2 WEEKS AFTER 911

War and Peace 9/11

October is a great month to visit Niagara Falls with its autumn colours and crisp sunny days. This marathon was one of the few to be held in two countries, starting in Buffalo in the US and then crossing the Peace Bridge into Canada, then along the Niagara River to finish at the Canadian horseshoe part of Niagara Falls. The race normally has a good balance of Americans, Canadians and other nationalities.

Sadly, the race did not start in America and had fewer Americans than normal. For a very good reason – the terrorist attack on the Twin Towers in New York a few weeks earlier on the 11th September. Americans were still in a state of shock after the first major terrorists attack in their country the government was not prepared to risk a possible attack on the Peace Bridge so the race was staged entirely in Canada with a new start near Lake Eyrie.

My Canada based sister, Avril, drove me down from Toronto to Niagara Falls where we stayed overnight in a local hotel. On the way down, we passed through some pleasant rural landscapes with some very nice vineyards producing a German Riesling type white wine. One small town close to Niagara had a very rustic atmosphere and old European style buildings, which was a pleasant surprise from many of the brash concrete and glass shopping malls of the New World. On the morning of the race, it was pouring with rain and we had a very trying 50km drive to the start. Before the race we met some Americans who had been bussed over from Buffalo, several of whom were from New York and had direct experience of the terrorist attack. It was a very emotional experience talking to these very friendly people, but as one of them said 'life has to go on and what better way to proceed than running a marathon in your neighbouring country'.

A few months earlier, I had a very enjoyable run in the Prague marathon and achieved a very good time for my age of 3hr 37 min. During August, I had some great coastal runs on paths along the beautiful Brittany coast in Western France. However, in September I had a return of a calf/Achilles tendon problem, similar to the one I had a year earlier in the Copenhagen and Lisbon marathons. I was probably under extra stress because I took up a new teaching post in September and so eased off training for a few weeks. I had also been dealing with a facial skin cancer that was operated on successfully in mid-September. I also missed a couple of vital long runs and this was a contributing factor to my subsequent below par Canadian marathon performance. I had already booked my flight to Toronto and my sister was really looking forward to my visit. There was no going back now.

Just before the marathon start, I put on a couple of elasticated bands to stop my Achilles from stretching too much and off we set in torrential rain. I wore a plastic rain sheet for the first few kilometres, which was a luxury step up from my normal bin liner with self-made holes for the arms. I kept negative thoughts of the rain and wet road at bay by having a conversation with a 35-year-old American man from Ohio. His target was 3hr 45 min, which surprised me in view of the fact that he was tall, over 13 stone and had a laboured way of running. I was not surprised when he had to pull up with a hamstring problem after about 10km. Running in shorts and little cover for his calves in cold wet rainy conditions did not help him. Later I got talking to another American also from Ohio who had already run an 18-mile section of the course in preparation. He had a heavy build and was finding the going tough and slowed down but ran non-stop to the end. I did manage to stay ahead of him – just. My Achilles stared to play up after about two hours. I adopted a run—walk—run method after about two and a half hours of non-stop running. At first I ran 3 telegraph pole lengths to one walking then it got down to one to one which was very frustrating .It soon became apparent that I was not going to make it in less than 4 hours. At about 39km stage a French Canadian girl came along side and guess what I got running again. It was pride, will power over injury and pain. She had run a 4hr 5 min marathon three weeks earlier and was hoping to break the 4-hour barrier. I told her that she should have left a longer rest period between marathons—at least six months so the body and mind can forget the pain of the last won. This must have encouraged her because she increased her pace and eased ahead of me. Oh how humiliating, and to think that I had run my last marathon in Prague in 3hr 36 min. I made a resolution then and there that this would not happen to me in my next marathon and I am pleased that in the following October in Budapest, Hungary, I got round in 3hr 46 min. As for our French Canadian, she just failed to get under 4hours, which is a pity because she finished quite strongly and maybe needed only to alter her race strategy to achieve her target. I finished in 4hr 5 min, cold and wet but uplifted by the roar and sight of the mighty Niagara Falls.

My sister drove me a few kilometres to her friend's house where I managed to have a nice long soak in a steaming hot bath. The lady of this house happened to be the one who had a bath in my sister's house in Toronto when on pulling a hand rail most of the tiles fell off the wall into the bath. However, at the time neither she nor my sister knew that I was the real culprit.

We had a very tough drive to get out of the Niagara Falls area because of dense fog but we arrived back in Toronto to a clear night sky.

My abiding memory of this marathon is meeting those wonderful New York runners and the support given to them by all the other runners. Peace is the only way forward.

THE THOMAS CORAM FOUNDATION OF LONDON

FOUNDLING GIRLS IN CHAPEL THOMAS CORAM FOUNDATION

This is the charity that I have raised the most funds for when participating in several London marathons. I was responsible in getting the charity involved in the London marathon and now each year several runners run the marathon in aid of The Coram Foundation.

Thomas Coram went to sea at the age of twelve and soon established a shipyard in Massachusetts and married a local girl from the city of Boston.

Returning to England at the age of 52, Coram was shocked at the sight in Georgian London of abandoned babies and young children left to die on dung heaps in the streets. It was a huge social problem. Outside the aristocracy, illegitimate children and their mothers were treated extremely harshly. Captain Coram started a 20-year campaign to obtain a royal charter from the king to establish the first Foundling Hospital for the maintenance and education of exposed and deserted young children.

The charter was granted in 1739 and the Coram Foundation is today the world's oldest incorporated charity independent of church and state.

PRESENTING CHEQUE TO DIRECTOR OF THOMAS CORAM FOUNDATION

The painter William Hogart , a friend of Thomas Coram, donated some of his works along with other artist to the foundation giving rise later to the birth of the Royal Academy of Arts. Handel was another benefactor. He gave concerts at the hospital to raise funds. In his will, he bequeathed a fair copy of his Messiah to the Founding Hospital.

Over two hundred years the foundling Hospital has looked after some 30000 children.

In 1926 the Foundling Hospital moved to Berkhamstead in Hertfordshire and was closed down in the early 1950s—some of its functions being replaced by the new National Health Service. The hospital became the first bi-lateral state school where I taught for 11 years. The school has kept its links with the Coram Foundation.

Today, part of the foundation's original London site is still in existence. The foundation is now comprised of the Coram Family, Coram Museum and Coram Fields—all at Brunswick Square.

Coram's Family services help vulnerable young people who have experienced trauma and family breakdown, or whose families are at risk. Support is given to one-parent families, families of mixed race and nursery education in and around London.

OTHER CHARITIES THAT I HAVE SUPPORT

National Society for prevention of cruelty to children (NSPCC)

Cancer Research

Anthony Nolan Bone Marrow Appeal

Delmaza House Hospice, Isabel Hospice

CORDA – coronary heart disease

Asthmatic Association

Africa small business project

Guys Hospital Kidney Appeal

"Politics is perhaps the only profession for which no preparation is thought to be necessary"

Robert Louis Stevenson

Conclusion: Marathon runners would not make good politicians

The Author

VIVE LA FRANCE

French marathons are let us say very French. They have that Gallic flair in terms of organisation and food—you will never get hungry whilst running in France.

4M PARIS MARATHON 15TH MAY 1988

Paris in the heat

As a reserve in case I did not get into the London marathon, I booked a place in the Paris marathon with a company called Sports Tours. I did get into the London but decided to run Paris as well even though it was only about 6 weeks afterwards. I broke the great American runner, Frank Shorter's maximum 'You have to leave enough time between marathons so as to forget the pain of the last marathon before you run the next one. Your mind must not know what's coming' He recommended six months as the minimum time needed between marathons.

This was to be my first of many marathons abroad, most of them organised by me which normally works out cheaper but the price offer by this sports company was hard to beat and besides it was nice to meet up with fellow runners (sufferers). We travelled by coach from London early Saturday morning and returned late Sunday evening staying just one night at a hotel near the inner Paris ring road.

The number of runners was less than half that of London and it lacked the atmosphere, fancy dress and crowd support of London. The French giant

BEATEN TO THE LINE RHE'MS 1998 RUNNING FOR NSPCC CHARITY

supermarket Carrefour sponsored the marathon. They supplied some tasty snacks along the marathon course and a nice goody bag at the end.

On the Saturday afternoon a fellow runner, a primary school head teacher, and I had time to explore the centre of Paris and ended up having a nice meal with a glass of red wine in the Latin Quarter. Soon we were on the metro back to our hotel and an early night.

I ran this marathon in support of the Corda Hearth Foundation. Little then did I know that I would need a double heart bypass 25 years later. They supplied my cotton running vest which was so full of sweat near the finish that I must have been one of the few marathon runners who weighed heavier at the finish than the start of the race!. It was a hot sunny day with a race start in front of Notre Dam cathedral and then a run up to the Arc de Triumph and on into the Bois de Boulogne. It was here that I some runners took short cuts but for me running is about yourself and there is no point in cheating yourself. My main problem was how to deal with the heat as the temperature reached the high 20s in the strong sunshine with little shelter from it. Thankfully, the fire brigade provided a cool shower at key points along the course. I also found the long straight avenues, some with cobblestones, a bit of a challenge. Surprisingly the finish was out in the eastern part of Paris and it seemed a very long time in coming. As we entered a park area, I could see a stadium through the heat haze in the distance, which was the venue for the finish. At least it would only be about 300meters on the track to the finish when I got to the stadium. I was wrong because when I got there and onto the hot black cinder track the grandstand finish looked still a long way in the distance and soon I realised that I was not in a running stadium but a venue for horse and cart racing and it was at least a kilometre on this hot track to the finish. The last 400 meters was like running on the surface of a hot range and a race photograph clearly depicts my distressed state. This finish turned out to my toughest in over fifty marathons. Luckily, I was able to lie down on a cool grass area for half an hour to recover. My time of 3hr 26 min was very satisfactory for me given the conditions.

I changed after a quick towel down—there were no shower facilities. We took the long coach drive to London and then the train to Hertford and finally to a long hot bath. From then on I did everything possible to make sure that I got a shower, or preferable a bath, soon after a race and avoid waiting several hours for that essential pleasure and reward for my exertions.

16 M CHERBOURGE FRANCE 1994

50 years on from the D-Day landings

The year 2004 was the only year when I ran four marathons within the year. Normally I aim to run two or three in a good year. After London in April, I decided to run two closely spaced marathons: Cherbourg on 2nd October and three weeks later the Abingdon Marathon in England as preparation for the 25th silver anniversary New York Marathon on 6thNovenmer. In retrospect, I should have left out the Abingdon marathon as it was only two weeks before the New York one. However, I did survive all these marathons and ran tall four under 3hr 40min, even though I did break my rule of leaving at least six months between marathons.

On the Friday evening, I left work and drove the stressful 100miles to Southampton docks to catch the overnight sailing to Cherbourg. Friday early evening is not the best time to go on the M25 London orbital motorway – or what is often termed Europe's biggest car park – but after nearly 4 hours, I made it to the port.

On board ship I had time for a meal and a few Guinness and then bed for a 6am wake up call. As we docked, I was surprised to see the port and town promenade bedecked in national flags but then I remembered that it was the 50th anniversary of the D-Day Normandy landings. A few months previously various heads of state visited Cherbourg, which was a key port that was captured in the D-Day landings.

As the race had only about 1000 runners I was able to book into a typical French small sea front hotel right next to the start/finish of the marathon. On the Saturday, I had a relaxing stroll around the town with a nice French fish soup and apple tart for lunch. This area is famous for its apples, most of which end up as cider or Calvados spirit. In the evening, we had the pre-race pasta party in a big Marquee near the beech front and then it was early to bed.

Race day was cool, dry and a little cloudy. These are ideal conditions to run a good marathon time. The course included quiet streets and some very nice open undulating countryside as well as a pleasant stretch along the beech. The only image of note that I have from the run is meeting two eccentric English men one dressed as a prison warden and the other one as his prisoner with ball and chain – made of plastic. I was to meet these men at the Belgium Antwerp marathon three years later. Towards the end of the race, I got talking in a mixture of French-English to a young Frenchman from Brittany and communicated enough to understand our joint Celtic origins. After the race as we walked towards the town centre and my Ferry in the distance, he suggested that I should come and spend a few days on his farm in Brittany. Alas I had to tell him that the ferry we could see would be taking me back to England in about two hours and there was a need for me to be back at school on Monday morning even though I would have loved to have gone for a visit to a real French home and experience some French hospitality. As for the my marathon time, I was happy with 3hr 30min but still would have liked to have broken the 3hr 30 min mark. At least I had an easy landing at Cherbourg unlike those young troops 50 years previously and I lived to tell the tail.

20M LA MARATHON DE REIMS October 1995

The Green Fields of France

The Champagne Trail

Having failed to qualify in my own right for the 100th Boston marathon in Helsinki I was hoping that a run in the Champagne region of France would put a bit of sparkle into my stride and help me qualify.

For this run, I joined a tour organised by Sportman's Travel who arranged for me to join a group of runners and their friends from the well know Mansfield Harriers Club in the north of England. I was to join their coach party at Dover at 8am so it was an early 4am rise for me to drive there and park up my car at the port. On getting into the coach I was somewhat taken aback by the 'Mickey taking' I got and that included the southern English coach driver. Maybe as a club, they resented an outsider joining them but I think my Irish name and the racist Irish jokes that permeated some sections of English society, including the media, had more to do with it. Of course the bombing campaign by the IRA did not help and the 800 year struggle between England and later the British for domination of Ireland made the Irish in Britain in their eyes fair game for 'mickey taking' or even shooting by some of their less controlled military representatives. I now look back and think that my first marathon in 1984 was not long after the death of 10 Irish hunger strikers and the blowing up of the some of the in power Conservative politicians in a hotel at their party conference in

Brighton. Relations between Ireland and Britain had reached another low point and tensions ran high. I am pleased that through out this difficult time that I had a very good reception to my marathon runs and got a very generous response for the charities that I supported. This was also the more rewarding when one realises that I thought in a very conservative English shire county and in schools with very few Irish. Since the' peace process' there has been a dramatic change in English attitudes towards the Irish and I am sure that members of today's Mansfield Harriers would give me a very different welcome than the one I got back in 1995.

We arrived early Saturday afternoon, registered for the marathon and then I made a point of visiting Reims cathedral – France's answer to Westminster Abbey. It was here that the Kings and Queens of France were crowned. Dusk was approaching and the interior of the huge cathedral was very eerie, lit only by candle light sparsely distributed around the naves. There were memorials to the fallen of the First World War that reflected the many war graves around Rheims. It always moves me when I visit the war graves and memorials of France and I cannot help but think about the huge waste and loss of young life. I had a similar reflective moment when I ran the Cherbourg marathon in Normandy in 1994 on the 50th anniversary of the D-Day landing nearby. In my view, the Second World War was a direct consequence of the stupidity of the First World War leaders – brave young men led by donkeys. I am reminded of the lyrics of the Irish folk song 'The Green Fields of France' and I quote just some of the lyrics here:

I see by your gravestone that you were only nineteen

When you joined the great fallen in nineteen sixteen

I hope you died well and I hope you died clean

Or Willie McBride ?—was it slow and obscene

. . . .

And did you leave a wife or a sweetheart behind

In some faithful heart is your memory enshrined

Although you died back in nineteen sixteen

In that faithful heart are you forever nineteen

. . . .

Well the sorrows, the suffering, the glory, the pain

The killing and dying was all done in vain

For young Willie McBride it all happened again

And again and again and again and again.

My melancholy mood was further enhanced by remembering some of the anti-war poems by Sassoon and Wilfred Owen that I learned at school. As I left the cathedral enshrouded in the mists of an autumn dusk it was time to go to rejoin Main Street with its lights and bars.

I saw an advertisement outside one bar for Murphy's Irish Stout so within a few minutes I had a glass of the black nectar in my hand. That was the good news; the bad news was that it cost me £3.50 or 5Euro. I cannot understand why French bars charge so much for beer and spirits especially when you can buy alcoholic beverages in French supermarkets for a fraction of the cost in the UK. My next drink was a glass of lemonade and then I departed for a nice oven baked pizza and some garlic bread for a real hydrocarbon load-up. Some of my Mansfield Harrier fellow travellers were in the restaurant but they kept to their own group, which suited me fine. Soon I was early to bed and oblivion.

The marathon organisers had put on several events that included a: 3k, 5k, 10k, 1/2 marathon and a relay which gave all ages a chance to participate. The marathon is not everyone's cup of tea—or should I say glass of Champagne. Sunday morning was cool and illuminated by a lovely Azure sky and by 10 am, I was on my way. I did a nice controlled run for the first 10km and then speeded up a little to reach half way in 1hr 41min – too slow to make it under 3hr 25min. I always run the second half marathon slower than the first half (one exception was the Nice marathon in November 2009). In training, there is a rule of thumb for predicting a marathon time. Providing you have trained up and done some 18-mile long runs, the rule is that you double your half marathon time and add 10 minutes. This would have given me a finishing time of 3hr 32min. I should have done the first half in 1hr 37min, still I ran on in hope and after 30km I was drifting beyond 5min per kilometre pace to finish in 3hr 32 min—7 minutes outside the Boston qualifying target.

On Monday, feeling surprisingly quite spritely, we visited the Taittinger Champagne cellars situated beneath the Abbey of St Nicoaise and dug out in the Gallo-Roman period. We saw some of the 19 million-bottle stock of Champaign. The aging process is about five years and there was a special reserved stock for customers who would be de-corking them to see in the new 2000 millennium – there were not cheap. Then, it was onto the coach back to Dover. I had a very nice chat with one of the club members on the coach in what was a much more tolerant and relaxed group of people, some of them even told me that they had Irish roots.

C'est la vie.

WINTER MARATHONS

14M ST ALBANS ENGLAND DEC 1993

ST ALBANS DEC 1993 WINTER MARATHON

A saintly run

December seems a strange month to run marathons in northern Europe and as expected they are not many available. Luckily, about 15 miles from where I live there was a marathon in St Albans – a small city famous for its cathedral and the roman ruins of Verulanium. The marathon was at the time was advertised as Britain's only winter marathon.

About 500 runners participated on a course that was a figure of eight shape centred on the main park in St Albans and taking in part of the suburbs of Hemel Hempstead to the north and Watford to the south. Most of the course was in open country and with some undulations.

Sunday 5th December was a lovely dry cool sunny day, perfect for running with a maximum temperature of 8C. Clad in my favourite Helle Hanson sweatshirt, outer T-Shirt, head-band and shorts, I was ready for the task ahead. It was only in later years that I resorted to elasticated leggings to keep hamstrings, calf muscles and Achilles tendons warm and dry.

Starting in the park with a fine view of the cathedral, we headed north into open countryside. I felt great and kept a steady pace throughout. As always, careful not to push to hard early on, 5 minutes per kilometre was my aim. There were few runners or spectators to consider except for the odd man and his dog, so there was plenty of time to enjoy the views and even count the sheep in the fields. In small marathons like this one your motivation comes from within and the knowledge that you have prepared well for the occasion. I was able to keep a steady pace, slowing as always in the last eight miles or so, to finish in 3 Hours 35 Minutes.

I drove home in about 45 minutes to a happy little daughter and a very tolerant wife. Within ten minutes, I was in a hot bath, always a real pleasure after a marathon. Whenever I am running abroad, I do my best to book a hotel room with a bath—not always easy. On the last stages of a marathon I keep going by visualising that lovely hot bath with soapsuds flowing over the edge. One of the great advantages of local marathons—now getting fewer—is that you do not have to get up at dawn to catch trains or buses and be there sometimes two hours before the start. Sadly, the St Albans marathon is no more. The cost of police patrols and health and safety regulations have proved to be the death knell of many local marathons.

A run in the woods

In the autumn of 2006, I had some time off before my next school contract so I was actively seeking a late autumn marathon. I considered running the Memphis Marathon in Tennessee, USA. About a week in the USA would be required, winter day light hours are shorter and it can be cold and rainy. I decided a visit in late spring or early autumn would be more enjoyable and on searching through the Marathon.Com website, I discovered to my surprise that there was a December marathon in Germany. The Siebengebirgen Marathon or the seven hills marathon in English, took place off road in a very hilly wooded district south of Bonn with great views over the Rhine river. When I looked at the profile of the course, it looked like a mini Alpine range with several hills involving climbs of up to 200meters. My first thought was that it would be madness to run this marathon; but then you have to be a little mad to run a marathon in the first place. This part of the German Rhineland is dear to me for two reasons. Firstly, the town of Bad Honnef in the Siebengebirgen was the first place I visited outside of Ireland and Britain when I was fourteen years of age. Secondly, my wife's stay at the nearby Bonn University allowed us to established two German family friends and this was an opportunity for me to meet up with them and enjoy their unmatched hospitality.

My first visit to the area was on a school trip from a school based in Kentish Town, London. I paid for the trip from the sale of a cow that I owned on our farm in Ireland. Six months prior to my school trip, we sold our farm and left for England. I had lived with my grandmother for eight years and rejoined my parents and siblings in London. My granny was able to buy a house in London with one of her sons who had left the farm some years before. The cow that I sold I had reared from a calf. It was a white calf when born and such albino type calves were not deemed to make good milking cows. With a bit of love, tender care and a lot of feeding, my calf grew up to be a fine-milking cow. With the money, I bought myself my first suit and paid for my school trip to Germany.

We stayed in a small hotel in Bad Honnef and went on river Rhine trips to Bonn and Cologne and forest walks in the Siebengebirgen. We also visited some open air swimming pools. The trip is very memorable for one particular incident. In 1962 Nike trainers had not been invented yet and for us kids polished leather shoes were the order of the day. Each morning, army style, we polished our shoes ready for inspection before leaving on our day trip. One morning whilst sitting on the edge of my bunk bed polishing my shoes, a piece of polish fell out of my polish tin and onto the whiter than white bed sheet. I tried to pick it off the sheet but it fell into small pieces and ended up as a black smudge. I did my best to conceal the smudge with the bed cover. That evening seated for supper—to my horror—the hotel manageress made a grand entrance to the dining room waving what appeared to be a large white flag above her head. She made straight to our Head Teacher and demanded to know which 'kinder' was responsible for destroying her valuable bed sheet – in German of course. A very embarrassed Head Teacher had to ask whose bunk the sheet came from. I could see that there was no way out and I stood up with all eyes on me, especially those of the manageress. A deep satisfaction came over the women – she had her victim. Job done. Surprisingly, the Head Teacher turned out to be quite conciliatory and I was spared the rod and only grounded for a day.

When I look back I am impressed to think that this school trip took place only 17 years after the war and to a part of Germany that was almost totally destroyed by Allied bombing and later invasion. Even then, one could see all around signs of rapid economic recovery that was to lead to the renewal of Germany as a world economic power rather than a military one.

I was prepared to make the extra effort to run this winter marathon because I knew that I would be provided with accommodation, food, wine and transport by our German friends who lived in Bonn. As part of her German and Linguistics degree, my wife, with our two young sons in tow, spent a year at Bonn University and early on in her stay was befriended by a couple of German students. Meckhild and Johannes were very supportive of my wife in her efforts to settle in the local community and also provided a little bit of social life. I can still remember my wife going with Johannes to see The Dubliners perform in the hallowed Beethoven Hall in Bonn. Meanwhile, I was helping Meckhild to settle into her Hall of Residence at Reading University where she had started a short course in English. A few months latter her parents came to stay with me in Reading in order to visit their only daughter. This was their first time out of Germany and it was especially memorable for Meckhild's father who had nearly died on the Russian front and then almost starved to death trying to escape the Russian westward advance towards the end of the war.

On the Saturday before the marathon, Meckhild and Johannes took me to the Bonn Christmas market and in the evening we went to a fine Italian restaurant. I must admit that I had a little more wine than normal not to mention an early couple of fine Bitburger lager beers. At least I knew that the beer must be good for me because all German beer is brewed under purity regulations that dictate the beer must only be brewed from natural ingredients. I was in bed by midnight but woke up a couple of hours later and thought 'am I mad to be doing this hilly marathon?' There and then I decided that I would lower my expectations and anything even under 5 hours would be an achievement.

We were up at 7.30 am, had a porridge breakfast and got to the starting place by 9.am. My German friends went off to a special memorial mass for Johannes's deceased parents nearby and would return later. I was on my own but the good news was that it was a glorious sunny frosty morning. We had pleasant kilometre walk in the forest to the starting point. There were about 700 runners in the race, all of them well winter clad. The first 7km was through flat valley floor land and very pretty it was. We then had a steep climb and I was walking by the 10km mark. Never have I walked so early in a marathon before. I thought I would be lucky to get under 5 hours at this rate of progress. But I got going again and reached the high point of the course several hundred meters above the river Rhine with a wonder full view 'Ausblick' of Bonn and even the famous spires of Cologne Cathedral in the distance. On the way up we met several German walkers who looked a little surprised to find people running uphill towards them. The Germans are great walkers and take pride in their long Sunday walks or in German ' Spazieren Gehen'.

I was very surprised to reach the half way stage in 2 hours and put this down to the hot tea and cakes that I received along the way. I found the downhill sections easy despite some mucky and stony paths. Some runners hate running down hill because it jars the knees. My technique is to increase my stride and speed and keep my nerve and just let go a bit. The same technique of letting go and not fighting the slope works for me in downhill skiing – if I can keep my nerve that is. The last 10km was very difficult and I had to use a run-walk strategy to get up some of the steep hills and got home in 4hr 13 min, my slowest marathon ever, but a great experience and a first on woodland footpaths.

Later I ended up in an Irish Pub to celebrate. However, on Monday I made up for this culturally when I went to the Guggenheim Museum in Bonn for a special exhibition of the work of Picasso.

Vielen Danken

33M PRAGUE INTERNATIONAL MARATHON 20ᵀᴴ MAY 2001

Handmade Crystal—handle with care.

When I think of Prague, I think of 1968. I remember that this was the year, when Russian tanks rolled into the city to suppress the growing democracy movement led by Dubcek. In 1968 my girl friend – soon to be my wife – and I were in charge of a bar and canteen at an international fruit picking camp near Wroxham in Norfolk. We had a 'Grapes of Wrath' moment when the majority of the fruit pickers who were mostly students from Eastern Europe went on strike for more pay. This paled into insignificance compared with what was about to happen in Prague.

PRAGUE OLD TOWN CLOCK AT FINISH

I was cleaning up the bar area one morning when a news flash came up on the television announcing the military invasion of Prague. It did not take long for the news to spread around the camp and soon there were scores of students in the bar. There was some tension between the Poles and the then Czechoslovaks because Polish troops were part of the invading forces. To ease the tension and defuse the situation we had to come up with a plan with the site-manager who agreed to my suggestion that we hire some coaches and get them down to the Russian Embassy in London to protest. It worked a treat. On their return from London, they were united now in their hatred of the Russians. They went to the bar for a joint celebration. The Czechs gave my wife some Czech dolls and miniature bottles of plum brandy and the Poles gave me a large glass of homemade potato spirit. They drank and sang into the early hours. The next day when I was cleaning the bar out I found the nearly empty forgotten glass behind a sherry barrel with a grey smear down the inside of the glass and a blackish gung of slush at the bottom. I was so busy the night before that I had no time to sample this Polish delight and had left it behind the sherry barrel for later sampling. It must have been at least 90% alcohol to judge by how much had evaporated—a lucky escape!

One of the outcomes of the Prague invasion was that many of the Czechoslovak students did not return home. It took the fall of the Berlin wall in 1989 before they could return and it took me 33 years before I got to Prague.

I was very fortunate that I travelled to Prague with a non-running friend who had worked for a few years as a quantity surveyor with British Aerospace who had a contract to build a new section to the city airport. He had happy memories of his stay in the city—particularly of the beautiful girls, inexpensive quality beer as well as the architectural beauty of the city itself.

As it was May and the asparagus season was at its highest, my wife gave me instructions to get a few bunches of her favourite vegetable and to get some of the famous Czechoslovak crystal – a nice salad dish would do fine. We met up with some of my friends former work colleagues in Prague and went for a meal on the outskirts of the city. A meal for eight people with several beers each cost only £20. During the meal, I mentioned that I wanted to buy some asparagus but I was not sure what the Czech word for the vegetable was. A woman member of the group thought that she knew what I was talking about and took me to a nearby garden centre where she showed me a bush-like evergreen plant. She was disappointed when I told her that it was nothing like what I was looking for. Back in the restaurant where the head waiter finally guessed correctly what I was looking for and it was called 'chesty' in the local language. He disappeared and after a while returned with a plate of cold cooked asparagus which of course I had to eat to show my appreciation. Needless to state that my wife never did get her bunches of asparagus but it was not for the want of trying. I had a little more success with the crystal search. After about two days of searching by a Czech colleague, I bought a large pedestal hand-cut crystal bowl with eight small matching pedestal fruit bowls. It cost £200 at that time but maybe five times more in England. To my amazement, my wife was not too pleased with my crystal set; she wanted something smaller and less elaborately decorated. Maybe I think I should have made a greater effort to bring back some asparagus.

I never knew that my night school German would come in so useful in Prague. Czechoslovakia was occupied in the Second World War by the Germans and later by the Russians. Middle-aged people learnt German and Russian at school instead of English so quite a few of the people that we met could communicate in German as my Czech was non-existent.

The marathon course was one lap passing over the famous Charles Bridge and river Vlada, past the castle through the new and old towns. Then on a long stretch upstream and back onto a lovely island and finishing in the new town—several hundred years old actually—with its famous clocks. The weather was fine and it was a case of running vest, shorts, headband, sunglasses and lashings of suntan cream. I had a very steady run and was able to keep going non-stop to finish the race in 3hr 37min that more than made up for my previous two marathons that were just over four hours.

We had time to visit the lovely Prague castle and the nearby city cathedral. Prague is famous for its classical music and its association with Mozart and other classical composers. I would have liked to have gone had to a concert but that will have to wait until the next time I visit the city with my wife so that she can sample the asparagus first hand.

35 M THE BUDAPEST MARATHON 29TH SEPT 2002

The not so Blue Danube marathon; but I got my China doll.

As with Prague my friend, Mike came with me to Budapest. He had never been to the city before but was hoping that it might be nearly as good as his beloved Prague. My wife took us to Heathrow starting at 4.30 am from our hometown of Hertford. It took some time to get Mike out of bed after a late night in his local pub. At the airport check—in there was a group of some 50 soldiers from the Green Howards regiment with very large kitbags ahead of us in the queue and I assume that they were going to Hungary as part of some military exercise, maybe to do with NATO.

There was only one think to do in order to get Mike quickly to the bar for some hair of the dog; so I asked one of the soldiers to take me to his commanding officer which he duly did. In my best commanding voice I asked the major if he would allow us to jump the queue as 'we' were going to run the Budapest marathon and that my friend needed to rest as he had only been able to sleep for a few hours. The major graciously received my request and ordered one of his troops to help us through with our luggage. I do not know what he thought as a very red bloated faced Mike was collected from the back of the queue and walked past on the way to the check-in; maybe the major thought Mike had been on a night training exercise carrying a large backpack. If he did not need a beer before Mike needed one now. Still I think he was impressed, if not embarrassed by my course of action.

I had a new contract teaching at Alleyn's school, part of the Dulwich college foundation and had given another assembly on my marathon exploits. More importantly, I elected to run the Budapest marathon to raise money for the school's elected charity which was The Delmelza House Children's Hospice, serving very sick children in the South East of England. One thinks of hospices as places for helping older people to die with dignity. It came as a quite a shock that such places existed for children. The motto of the hospice was

'The hospice focuses on adding life to days when days cannot be added to life'.

As we arrived mid-morning on the Saturday we had time to visit Beckett's Irish pub and down 5 pints of Guinness – I had to keep up with Mike. That evening I had a good pasta meal and plenty of water and then early to bed. Mike preferred to stay on in the company of some barmaids. I was determined to run a sub 4 hour marathon as I failed to do so in my previous marathon at Niagara Falls in Canada and this time I had no calf muscle or Achilles tendon problems. The course was a single loop course, which I prefer, and with several bridges to cross over the Danube river. It also included a run on a lovely island in the Danube and a run past the Hungarian parliamentary building in the latter part of the race. The building reminded me of the UK Houses of Parliament, very gothic in design and built in the 19th century.

The weather was fine and sunny but not too hot. The first 3km from Heroes' Square took us past the Opera House and towards the famous chain bridge across the Danube. I got talking to a couple from London who had links with the well-known Enfield Harriers Club. The woman partner wanted to break 3.20 from a previous best of 3.40 with her male partner acting as her pacemaker. Despite the blue sky, the Danube had a light grey hue, maybe Mozart's blue Danube only applies to the part of the river in Vienna. With an aiding nice cool breeze, we ran several kilometres along the river in very bright sunshine. I was glad that I was wearing sunglasses. There was also a relay race in conjunction with the marathon that provided me with a bit of extra pace making and I stayed close to 5km/min pace. I got to half way in 1hr 47min so a sub 4-hour time was now a real possibility. I got through my key times of 2.11 and 3.11 non-stop but by 36km I walked at a drinks station for the first time, but got going again; but struggled again at 40km where my extra thirst often sets in. Still I managed to finish with a bit of a sprint in 3hr 46min. Job done. I took the metro and a 1km walk got me back to my hotel and a long hot soak in the bath. We did our usual pub visits and the next morning spent some time at the castle where I purchased a china doll to add to my collection. Mike thought my china doll was nice but was disappointed with the girls of Budapest—he is a hard man to please. I did regret that I visited the famous Turkish Baths of the city. Maybe there will be a next time.

43M POZNAN MARATHON POLAND Oct 2006

The happy teacher.

Since the fall of the Berlin Wall in 1989 there has been a large influx of eastern Europeans to the UK, the largest group by far coming from Poland. The first wave of Polish immigrants or refugees came to the UK at the beginning of World War 2 and included a large number of Polish military fleeing from the German invasion of their country. The UK had a treaty with Poland that in the event of a German declaration of war on Poland, the UK would come to their aid so it was natural that many Poles would try to find their way to the UK in the event of war. The Polish army put up a brave defence against the overwhelming German land and air attack and soon the capital Warsaw was in German hands. One consequence of the invasion was that many of the leading core of Polish army and air force officers managed to escape the country and find there way to England via Turkey and Spain. They formed their own Polish air and land units as part of the Allied war effort and made a very significant contribution in the fight against Nazism. I had the privilege of having one of these former Polish officers as a neighbour in Hertford and he was one of the many who did not go back to Poland after the war, as their country was effectively under Stalinist Russian control. If they did go back, they faced execution or a long stretch in Siberia.

The new wave of post cold war Polish immigrants, like their predecessors soon acquired a reputation for hard work, honesty and reliability. They came in their hundreds of thousands to the UK and Ireland. I can remember in 2005 meeting five different Polish workers in one day: one in a Photoshop, another in a coffee shop in London, one in a restaurant in Hertford and another serving in my local pub. The fifth Pole I met was a young woman who knocked on my door selling some of her artwork and I bought a very nice sketch of a cat that she had drawn.

Ireland has a long relationship with Poland in the field of soccer matches between the countries since the Second World War. Maybe it was the strong Catholicism and struggle for national identity that brought them together. In a recent friendly soccer match in Dublin (2008) Poland beat Ireland 2-0 in front of at least 20,000 migrant Polish workers – it was almost like a home game for Poland. It is also no coincidence that the Irish airline Ryanair has established regular routes to key Polish cities. I took a Ryanair flight from London to Poznan for my first Polish marathon adventure in October 2006. I believe that, on a full plane, I was the only Irish passenger on board as it is mostly only Poles that travel between Ireland and Poland.

Poznan is a city about half way between Berlin and Warsaw that put it in direct line for both Russian and German invasions and in consequence, the city was nearly all destroyed in the Second World War. I took a taxi from the airport into the city and, as in my previous trip to Prague, my basic German came in useful because the Polish taxi driver could speak German—he had worked in a German factory for some years. I sensed from him that there was still some animosity between the Poles and the Germans after centuries of conflict; but football was the main topic of our conversation.

The evening before the marathon, I attended Mass at a Carmelite Monastery and was surprised to find I was one of the oldest people in the church. Most of the fifty plus monks were younger than me as was most of the congregation. As a baby in Ireland, I was dedicated to a Carmelite Order in Wicklow where my great aunt was a nun. I had always thought that only women became Carmelites after their founder St Theresa of Liseux in France.

My spiritual needs satisfied, I found a restaurant that served an excellent cheap pasta meal that set me up nicely for the marathon next morning.

Race day was dry, dull, cool, crisp and autumnal – excellent conditions for long distance running. The race started near to a modern international rowing regatta centre and was some 5km form my hotel, so I took a taxi and walked the last 2km along the lake to the start. The course was two laps—not my favourite – but mostly flat with one long incline. A few thousand runners participated, the vast majority coming from Eastern Europe. The first 3km of the race led back to the cobbled streets of the city centre and then along a wide dual carriageways out to a few kilometres of open country and then back to the start. On the second lap, I decided to discard my plastic bin liner – my rain and cold insurance garment of choice – when a Polish runner noticed the oddity of the plastic bag and the fact that I was from the west from my now exposed running vest. We got talking and ran the rest of the race together.

He was a Polish further education college lecturer from the city where the great astronomer Copernicus was born—Torun (Thorn). His monthly salary was equivalent to a classroom teacher's weekly salary in the UK, but he could live and support a family on this as long as he did not holiday in the West. As we ran past some grim communist period blocks of flats, he remarked that he used to live with his parents and siblings in a similar flat. They often had to wait five years to get a TV, but if production quotas were not achieved, they could be offered a fridge instead. A car was out of the question. I do not think that he had any regrets about the passing away of the Soviet led communist era.

We finished the marathon together in 3hr 56 min and were pleased to break the 4-hour mark. It was probably one of the most relaxed marathons that I have run, greatly helped my talking to some interesting runners with similar finishing targets and running within their limits.

On Sunday evening the centre of town was very quite and I had to settle for a posh restaurant – one of the few open – in the main square and was amazed to find prices were similar to top London eating establishments. The hourly wage of the student waitress was about £1 whilst a starter cost £6. I noticed that there were not too many people in the restaurant and those that were there confined themselves to one course. Like other neighbouring east European countries, you have to have places for the growing number of super rich to dine in.

Copernicus had opened up the way for humanity to understand the solar system and to explore the heavens free of the hold of Christian orthodoxy. Our teacher in Torun is now part of the new Poland, free of Stalinist repression, and free to help Poland towards new horizons.

GOING DUTCH

9M ROTTERDAM MARATHON March 1991

World Record Course

I have run two marathons in the Netherlands. This first marathon was one of the coldest with snow showers and the second one in Leiden in June 2007 was the hottest of all my marathons. The Rotterdam marathon is a fast flat course with some of it below sea level and it came as little surprise that the Etopian Balayneh Densimo broke the world marathon record here in 1988 in a time of 2hr 6 min 50 sec. The women's winner was Chinese and the Chinese women were to take the first three places in the 10km at the Olympics the following year. In fourth place was Sonja O'Sullivan of Ireland who had been the favourite. The Chinese winners were never participated in competition again. I am pleased to say that Sonja did win a silver medal at a later Olympics but many people suspected foul play in the preparation of the Chinese athletes.

The race started in the afternoon and I was able to watch the start of the London marathon on TV. Like Sweden and despite their liberal tradition Dutch Lutheranism still has a hold on the nations Sabbath activities in this part of the Netherlands – at least in the morning.

I had met a very nice Dutch family on my regular visits to Norway—they had a mountain cottage (hytte) near where my sister-in-law lives in Hallingdal. They invited me to stay with them in the medieval university town of Leiden. Leiden was the last port of call of some of The Pilgrim Fathers from England as they sailed to the New World. There is a memorial plaque to them in the local cathedral, which is now used for open markets, as was often the case in medieval times.

On Saturday night I went on a bike ride with Mickel – who I had skied and 'smoked' with on several occasions in Norway—to the town centre and downed a few strong beers. Luckily, for me the Dutch only drink beer in small glasses.

On Sunday, Mickel and I took a late morning train down to Rotterdam, a quick change in the lobby of the Hilton hotel and I was on my way.

The course was a figure of eight that took in a royal park with an avenue named Queen Astrid – a nice reminder of our daughter Astrid Colleen then aged 5 years – some of the dock area and the modern Philips Football Stadium that is home to the football club PSV Eindhoven. The roads were wide and thankfully had few cobblestones. Conditions were cold with intermittent sunshine and snow showers. I noticed after the race that my neck and arms were a bit sunburnt, which surprised me in view of the cold. I was to get sunburn again in similar conditions in the 97th Boston marathon. I was a slow learner when it came to using suntan cream. The race itself was uneventful and I was very pleased with my time of 3hr 23min.

I had the usual problem of getting back to England for work on Monday morning but my Dutch host had thoughtfully pre-booked a full Indonesian meal, which was very enjoyable. I left Teepol airport about 7pm. At the airport, I remembered Michel's Dad having a go at him about his chain smoking. Sadly, his Dad died a few years ago.

46M LEIDEN MARATHON 10TH JUNE 2007.

Not so charged by The Leiden Jar.

I can still remember from my schools days the Leiden Jar, a device that helped literally to put a spark into our Physics lessons. The Leiden jar was invented in Leiden, an ancient university city in the Netherlands, and consisted of a glass jar with an inner and outer metal layer which allowed it to store electric charge. On touching the inner metal surface you could receive quite an electric shock. Sometimes if it was well charged up you could put a finger near to the jar and a spark would travel to your finger which would certainly wake you up.

I had already stayed in Leiden with Dutch friends in 1991 when I ran the Rotterdam marathon. This time I stayed with a Belgium friend in Antwerp and travelled up by train on the Sunday morning for the race which started in the early afternoon. We had to take three different trains, but most of the journey was on a Double Decker train that allowed for a great view of the surrounding Dutch countryside and towns. Normally my friend would have driven me but his car needed repair. He extolled the virtues of taking the train but I did notice that when he got his car back a few days later it was like being back again with a long lost love – he even drove the few hundred meters to the local shops in Antwerp. Sometimes necessity can make people think outside the box, but most of us soon revert to our old ways when we regain the luxuries of modern living.

Normally I would not run a marathon in June and especially the day before my birthday, but I had finished a teaching contract at The City of London Girls' School at the end of April so I was free to do some extra training. Unfortunately I had a bit of an ongoing cold virus for 3 weeks in May which meant at least 8 days of no training but I did manage to put in a 26 mile and 18 mile week in the two weeks prior to the marathon. I knew this was a bit late in the day but still very necessary for me. Several sessions in the gym pool helped to raise my general fitness and stamina level.

We arrived at Leiden station 40 minutes before the start and walked a kilometer to the church, which was, unusually, the venue for final race registration. It was a beautiful hot sunny day with a slight breeze and inside the church was very humid and I was already sweating. A nice day for a swim but not for running and my confidence was somewhat dented when I heard that the Amsterdam marathon at the end of April was hit by a heat wave and was officially called-off half way through the race with runners continuing at their own risk. Could Leiden be a repeat? I slapped on lashings of factor 50 suntan lotion and with just running vest and shorts, my Nike shoes, socks, headband, cap and sunglasses I was ready for the off.

he route was flat and was over two laps: along old cobbled streets, country lanes through Frisian cow grazing pastures and canal paths. Most of the runners were sensible and were only doing the half-marathon one lap. The starting temperature was about 24 Celsius and rising. The first lap was enjoyable, scenic and well supported by spectators and bands along the route. However, there is always a temptation to keep up with the faster half marathon runners and I am pleased to say that I kept my own pace to get to the half way mark in 1hr 55min, which was a little too slow to be sure of getting under 4 hours.

The second lap was much tougher with the temperature at 27 Celsius and very strong sunshine and little shelter. It was not long before I had to start my strategy of run-walk-run. I made sure to run where the number of spectators was greatest to tap into there support which was now fuelled by copious amounts of Heineken lager. At 35km, my only thought was to finish the marathon. ly I got talking to a young Dutch student which took my mind to some extent off the heat and physical effort. As the runners were now fewer in number, the bands were able to give us an extra blast to help us on our way and we were sprayed a plenty from kids using their garden hosepipes. In the last two kilometers, one attractive black girl band singer noticed that I was walking and was having none of it. After a great cheer from her, sheer embarrassment got me going again all the way to the finish. My sprint finish was maintained by the public commentator singling me out for special attention.

I needed at least 30 minutes to cool down but soon a couple of lagers were restorative. We had a long delayed train journey back to Antwerp for a few more beers in Kelly's Irish Pub, followed by a good meal in an Argentinean steak house and finally a lovely hot bath at 11pm at my friend's apartment. It was a long day out and my batteries were fully discharged. A good night's sleep quickly recharged my system and I can remember dreaming about my laboratory experiments with Leyden Jars and Van de Graff Generators and sparks flying everywhere.

*"There is a time to run and a time to rest.
It is a true test of the runner to get these right"*

Noel Carroll

SWISS AND NOT ON TIME

48M ZURICH SWITZERLAND 20TH APRIL 2009

Higher than I thought.

From a running perspective, this marathon defeated me. I failed to achieve the modest target of running it in under 4 hours. This was despite my preparations being adequate and a very favourable race day for running.

April in Zurich is a very pleasant time of year, especially after a cold winter in this alpine land. Race day was sunny, cool and there was an early 8.30am start. I did not have to get up too early because a special bus picked runners up from our hotel and drove us from the centre the 5km south along the lake to the start. Zurich is situated at the head of a large lake called 'Zurich See', so the course involved running up to Zurich centre on the west side of the lake and then a much longer run of about 15km down the east side of the lake to return back the way we came to the finish. It was a very scenic route with constant views of the lake and surrounding snow capped mountains. There were only two longish uphill climbs to cope with.

This was also one of the few occasions that I did not spend Easter in Norway – my wife's country, so that left me some time to run a bit more in England's green and pleasant land. I put in four consecutive weeks of: 22, 25, 25 and 18 miles prior to the marathon. Added to this were several swimming sessions and some bike and cross-trainer work in my local gym. Again, I failed to do any serious long runs. My longest runs were two runs of 1hour 25min. By my standards—even at the age of nearly 62—this training schedule should have been sufficient to achieve a sub four hour marathon. I also had no injuries or sickness to concern me.

The night before the marathon, I had a very substantial Italian meal, made all the more enjoyable by a good conversation with a Swiss couple sitting at the next table to mine. The husband was a member of the Swiss national parliament. He was very much to the political nationalist right and wanted much tougher laws on anti-immigration. I noticed that even his wife was keen to distance herself from his views at times during our conversation. Still we covered quiet a few political topics to such an extent that I consumed a half bottle of wine to enhance my German speaking skills. Normally I take some wine or beer before a marathon in the belief that a little bit of alcohol helps thin the blood. At my age, one never knows what could happen during a marathon. Of course, one could take a little aspirin to achieve the same ends; but wine tastes much better.

I was in good time for the start of the race. I had a pleasant stroll along the lakeshore with time to take in the wonderful view of the snow-capped Alps in the distance. The Swiss are quite an inventive race and I was amazed how they used numbered railway carriages to hold the belongings of some 10,000 runners involved in the race. I decided to run in my usual leggings and running vest. I started at a good pace but I felt a little warm despite the cool lake breeze. I had to wring my headband of sweat every kilometre. Maybe it was the wine I had the night before; but I reasoned it had more to do with the strong sunshine along with the higher altitude. Anyway, that is my excuse for sweating so much.

I ran past four Swiss men in national costume blowing on long mountain horns, so long that the ends rested on the ground. They emitted a sound that echoed through my head. This forced me to give my headband another good wringing. There was very little banter amongst the runners. Well I was in Switzerland where they take their running seriously. Consequently, I had plenty of time to enjoy the scenery and to keep my eye on my time splits. I reached the half waypoint in 1hr 52min, which put me in line for a sub four marathon. By now, I was feeling unusually fatigued and mentally a little negative. At 30km running against a bit of a breeze, I walked to take a drink. Some music from a local band helped me to get going again. By now, most of the leading runners had passed us on the way back to the finish. There was the usual strong African representation in the leading pack. I did notice one very pale red haired Russian in the leading group and was very surprised to learn later that he had won the marathon.

I now resorted to my normal routine tactic of tucking in behind other runners to shield me from the wind and to focus on their backs and not the long open stretch of open road ahead .Again I had to walk a bit and then find some passing runners to tuck in behind and get going again. I do not like having to run like this but needs must.

I was now very conscious that the clock was getting the better of me and that my sub 4-hour target was becoming more of a dream as the minutes passed. As the great German philosopher Goethe said 'time waits for no man'. As Switzerland is the home of the clock, this was the last place in the world to try to beat the clock!

Normally to get under 4 hours at my age I have to run the first half in about 1hr 52min (which I did) and keep running until at least the 34km marker. Towards the end of a marathon it is possible to delude oneself that you are still running at your earlier pace and speed. I managed to keep running to finish in 4hr 2min. Still there was some reward from a quick train journey back and then a nice long soak in a hot steaming bath.

Upon reflection, I think there could be another reason why I felt so lethargic in the second part of the race. In January, I took on a full time teaching post at St Edmund's College – the oldest catholic school in England and a former seminary. It was the first time in 37 years that I had taught at a catholic school. I was standing in for an ill Head of Physics and there was an enormous amount of work to do in terms of teaching, laboratory organisation and staff support. I found the challenge along with the freedom of action quite uplifting but exhausting. I was on the move all day long in a hot house of human interaction

I think that this job depleted my physical and mental reserves more than I had realised. Long distance running is as much about mental fitness and stamina as physical preparation. If I look at my marathon times over the years the more stress I was under at work the slower my times. I think one can risk injury if you do not get the right balance between work, training and play.

I took the last plane back to London to arrive home at 1 am and was at work at 8.30 am. Sadly, it was not long before Zurich was a distant memory.

STOP PRESS. Later on, I checked up on the altitude of Zurich above sea level and discovered that it is 820 meters! As I was training and living at sea level, it is quite likely that running at this fairly high altitude could explain some of my relatively poor second half marathon performance.

FROM THE BALKANS TO THE BALTIC

49M LJUBLJANA MARATHON, SLOVENIA 26TH OCT 2008

Irish wakes and Slovenian horse burgers at 3 euro each.

My knowledge of Slovenia prior to this marathon was very limited. I knew that it was a place where one could go skiing, had a population of about two million inhabitants and was part of Tito's former Yugoslavia. Compared to other former eastern—bloc communist countries it was relatively prosperous. As I had already run in Estonia, one of the newly liberated Baltic States, it seemed a good idea to go to the Balkans and run in a newly liberated Slavic state.

The year 2008 was sadly a year when I attended eight funerals; five of the deceased were younger than me. In 2008 I was at that age when funerals outnumber christenings and weddings. A week prior to this marathon I attended the funeral of my aunt in Ireland who I am pleased to say died peacefully in her sleep at the age of 86 years. The Irish know how to do funerals and this was my second Irish funeral and wake within a year. When I die, I hope my family will do an Irish wake for me with plenty of booze of course. (There is now a new tradition emerging, if you know that your time is soon to be up and you are still physically and mentally ok, one can have a pre-wake wake so you do not completely miss out on your own wake as it were). This will be over my open coffin at home hopefully with many a slante and recaps of

LJUBLJAN MARATHON SLOVENIA 2008 HORSE BURGER 3 EURO

my own exploits on the boozing front and even a mention of a few marathons thrown in. I hope I will be able to join them in a spiritual reunion from beyond the Pearly Gate. My favourite biblical miracle is the Feast of Cain when the Good Lord converted water into wine. With the prices of spirits in Norway I could have done with the Lord's help in years gone by. Nowadays we have the supermarkets and cheap pub chains like Weatherspoons in the UK to help us through our feasts and celebrations.

On the first night of a wake there is a relatively restrained alcoholic intake with tea, coffee and plenty of sandwiches also available. It is important that there is always someone present with the departed one throughout the night. The next evening the body is taken to the church and there is a short service. The body lies in state over night until the funeral mass next morning and then burial. Most of the evening mourners return to the family home for part two of the wake to celebrate and regale the departed one into the early hours.

It was part two of my aunt's wake that I stayed up most of the night, despite knowing that I was running a marathon in Slovenia a week later. Funerals have a melancholy effect on me and make me very aware of my own mortality and the fact that you only live once—this even despite the possibility of re-incarnation.

The autumn 2008 found me free of a teaching contract. At that time I was not sure if I wanted to return again to the chalk-white board after 40 years teaching in a wide range of schools. I did return in 2009 for a short teaching contract at the end of the spring term. I feel that I have done my duty and I am very thankful for all the wonderful experiences, trials and tribulations that I have had in the world of education. Teaching in the company of young people for so long can make you feel a bit like Peter Pan; but as Goethe said 'time waits for no man'.

With no teaching commitments my training for the Slovenian marathon was a very relaxed affair with my usual failure to put in a long run over 1hr 45 min., but I felt confident I could get under four hours after my failure to do so in Zurich earlier in May of that year. I arrived in Ljubljana early Friday evening in order to allow time for a little partying before Sunday's race. On the mini-bus from the airport – only 5 euro – I met a Scotsman who told me that he had entered to run the marathon but because of injury, he had to pull out; but as he had paid for flight and hotels he would take a bit of holiday in the country instead. I suggested we meet up later for a drink, but was surprised when he told me that he wanted to meet real Slovenians – the cheeky sod. I made up my mind there and then that I would meet Slovenians as well and outdo him. Normally I end up meeting the locals on my marathon trips, even if I start in an Irish Pub. I never make a point of doing so from the start as I often get some good local knowledge and tips on the area in Irish pubs. I prefer an organic approach and let events dictate the evening.

After I checked in to my hotel I had a stroll around the small but quant city centre. I noticed a restaurant that sold 'horsemeat burgers' at 3 euro and with a big picture of a work horse on the window. Most English people would be horrified at the idea of eating horsemeat. The horse burger restaurant reminded me of the horse that we had on my grandmother's farm in Ireland.

The horse's name was ' Jacksiepanama' and was halfway between a shire and a race horse in terms of strength, size and speed. I was a bit of a wild lad and frequently rode Jackiespanama at a full gallop with no saddle or halter. I guided him by tapping on the left or right side of his head and controlled his speed with my legs and I always had one hand holding on to his mane. No health and safety rules to worry about in those days. I did not learn from the accident I had when as a six year old I crawled up behind a pony who lashed out with both rear hooves and caught the back of my head on the return. Luckily he did not get me on the lash out otherwise I would have met my maker sooner than planned. As well as for pulling carts we used Jacksiepanama to pull in cocks of hay from the hay field to build big ricks of hay in the farm yard. One connected a chain round the base of the cock of hay and connected the ends to the horse's halter and the pull of the horse would slide it along the ground. My job was to sit on the top of the cock of hay and guide the horse with the rains. Once I fell forward and the heavy load of hay was nearly pulled right over me but I managed to grab one of the side chains at the last moment to pull myself clear and lived to tell the tale. We also used Jacksiepanama to pull a large metal rack to rack up the hay off the ground into long lines to dry out and needless to say I had a few lucky escapes operating the rack to make sure that I did not get racked up as well. The day came when we had to sell the farm and to leave Ireland and Jacksiepanama who was getting on in years. As was the practice then the horse was sold and exported live to Belgium where he probably ended up as horse salami burgers. Incidentally they still eat horse salami in Norway which is a very dark, dry and quite tasty meat, especially with a good dash of mayonnaise. Some horses were also locally slaughtered to feed the hounds used for foxhunting.

At that time – the late 1950s – a British tabloids decided to 'expose the cruelty' suffered by Irish horses transported live on ships to Belgium. Personally, I have no objection to eating horsemeat but I do not agree with live transportation. Ironically the Irish government would have got more value added by slaughtering and preparing the horse meat in Ireland. The same applied to live cattle transported to Britain at that time,

I think that as Ireland was economically isolated in the 1950s they could not afford the infrastructure and like many African countries today export the raw materials to be processed elsewhere. I also believe that Britain received both live cattle and horses for consumption from Ireland during the second world, which they were very glad to receive and did not allow any moral qualms to get in the way. I suppose one can take the moral high ground more easily after the horse has bolted!

After a beer in an almost empty British styled pub I decided to return to my hotel for a snack. My hotel was a converted eastern European 15 storey block of flats with no balconies and I would rate it as 2star; but it was close to the centre and there were few other hotels to choose from. Close by I espied another block of flats with some shops and a bar at ground level and took the opportunity to take a locally brewed beer. The beer came in half-litre bottles but as I have never been one to make the publican's life too easy I insisted on having a glass and not drinking straight from the unwashed bottle like the locals. I prefer a nice thin rimmed glass, first to see the beer and its head and then to feel and sip the amber nectar without a mouthful of thick glass to contend with. For me sight and taste go together. When it comes to matching the right glass to different types of beer, Belgium is my dream country. Whilst ordering my beer with glass a local heard me speak English and immediately offered to treat me. It turned out that he had spent six years working in Ireland and his brother was still working there as a hotel manager in Cork. After a few more beers we agreed that Slovenian girls were prettier than Irish girls and that Slovenian beer got better with each bottle that was consumed. We adjourned to another bar where we met big Boris and his wife and friends and by now I was well into Slovenian bar social life. I was quite pleased that I had asked Boris first before dancing with his very beautiful wife as Boris could be quite the jealous type. Finally I can remember meeting some students along the river bank at about 3am. After sharing a beer or two with them, I decided to show how good at pull-ups and press—ups I was only to slip and give myself a nasty black eye. They kindly helped me back to my hotel and I was in bed by 4am. Saturday was going to be a long lie in, no alcohol and then a good pasta meal and bed by 9.30 pm. I often wondered how the Scotsman got on that evening. As for me, I certainly met and mixed with the locals.

Sunday morning I was up at 7am – a new man –especially after a good breakfast. A nice stroll to the start and we were off at 10am. A part from a chat with two American girls doing the half marathon they were very few distractions from enjoying the sights along the two lap course which took in some nice alpine type country scenes that included a few horses as well as cattle. The weather was coldish and quite dull with little wind—excellent weather for running—and I was pleased to finish in 3hr 52min.

I had a very pleasant meal with wine in moderation on Sunday evening; but I still have some regrets of not trying one of those horse burgers.

50M RIGA MARATHON LATVIA 17TH MAY 2009

From Russia with Love.

It was the British Prime Minister when asked what made for interesting politics, stated 'Events dear boy' or words to that effect. So it was 'Events' that lead me to Latvia for my **50th marathon running in my 30th country.**

I would have liked to run a marathon in Africa as my 50th; but the marathon that attracted me—the Kilimanjaro – was in March and would have involved a stay in Nairobi, which was far too dangerous and too hot for me. Also I could not resist the opportunity to go to Dublin in late February for an Ireland versus England rugby match in what turned out to be a 'grand slam' year for Ireland after their last one 61 years earlier in 1948 when I was two years old. However I did have a reason for selecting Latvia because I went to neighbouring Estonia in 2008 to run a marathon only to find that it was cancelled 48 hours before the start because of some issues with the Estonian Russian organiser and local native Estonians – ' Events dear Boy' as MacMillan would have put it. We did get the opportunity to run a 10km race in a nice wooded area near to the sailing base used as part of the Moscow Olympics in 1980. I had my Belgium fan club with me – Jacques and Robin—and managed 4 pints of excellent Estonian lager in the hours before the race and therefore was able to enjoy the company of an Estonian middle-aged teacher and was pleased to be able to help her to a PB for this distance. I was also glad that the marathon was cancelled in some ways as I went to the wrong airport and missed my plane out on the Friday morning. Instead, I had to go out early Saturday morning. I would have had to run the marathon a few hours after arrival on the Saturday afternoon

May is a good month to run in northern Europe and to run on the 17th May being the Norwegian National Day was even better for me. I was also keen to complete a marathon in one of the three newly liberated Baltic Republics. The three Baltic countries of Estonia, Latvia and Lithuania share a common history of periods of invasion and domination by their bigger neighbours in the 20C particularly Russia and Germany.

The Latvian population has been multiethnic for centuries. In 1897 the first official census indicated that the country's population was comprised of 68% ethnic Latvians, 12% Russians, 6% Germans and 4% Poles. After the First World War and the formation of an independent Latvia, there was an increase of ethnic Latvians to 77% of a total population of 1.9 million. The Second World War brought first a German occupation followed by a more devastating Russian invasion involving war casualties, deportations and emigration so that by the end of the cold war in 1989 ethnic Latvians now only comprised 52% of the population with a Russian population of 27%. The 1980s was a period of national awakening primarily to the fear of being a minority in their own country; this fear was encapsulated in the rallying cry 'Now or Never'. In 1991 after a stand off with elements of the Russian army Latvia declared independence and this move is represented today by a very impressive 'Freedom Monument' in the centre of Riga. Despite a history of occupation, Riga old town retains its Hanseatic architectural heritage and part of the city wall is still in tact with many cobbled streets and churches aplenty.

I was able to savour some of the culture and lifestyle of the city by spending some hours with a local Latvian 20 year old girl called Alyssa who had spent a year in Norway with one of my wife's relatives. Her father was a director of a company that represented the new capitalist and entrepreneurial spirit of modern Latvia. She did not have much empathy with Russian Latvians and told me that even I could recognise them after a couple of days in the city and she was right because the Russians seemed to serve in most of the bars and restaurants in the city. On one occasion in a late night bar I got talking to a Russian barman and he showed me his 'Latvian passport' with the word Russian stamped on it and whilst he was proud of his Russian origins he felt that he was being discriminated against. As for Alyssa, she was going to study business at the university and follow in her father's footsteps. There would be no bar work for her. She was also going to run the 5km race but alas dropped out. I hope her enthusiasm for business will not be so fickle. Even after a session with Alyssa in the local Irish pub the day before the marathon – she drank water – I still found it hard to relate to her and her very reserved viewpoints. Still she was a bit of an optimist because upon finding my marathon result in the local paper she emailed me to say that she would be running the marathon the following year. I think she should try the 5km first.

Prior to going to Latvia I had read several reports from Irish and British visitors that they did not find the locals too friendly and that they were an 'unsmiling lot'. I have to say I did detect certain sullenness in some people which could have been a hang over from the grim communist era when customer service was not a priority. I do not think that the behaviour of visiting stag parties endeared the locals to foreigners, especially when some of them were arrested for relieving themselves on the new Freedom Monument.

The marathon course was a two lap affair which is not my favourite course with a special extra section for marathon runners through a derelict industrial area with uneven cobbled streets—the most unsafe road surface that I have ever run on. Otherwise, the rest of the course and organisation was good as was the weather – cool and cloudy. A group of Italians from a Rome running club who were running the half marathon enlivened the race atmosphere. I certainly missed them on the second lap, which was a bit lonely and a bit of a struggle. Still I was please to break the four-hour mark and come home in 3hr 58 min.

That evening I hit the town for a meal and a few drinks and met several locals both Russian and ethnic Latvian. Some Russian girls were very free in passing their Vodka around and an ethnic Latvian and I got arrested for drinking in public which I was not aware was an offence, still ignorance of the law is no excuse. The next day I paid my fine and headed for the airport and that was my 50th marathon.

EDINBURGH – TURBAN CHARGED SIKHS

41M EDINBURGH MARATHON JUNE 2005

'Wha's like us? Damn few and they're a'deid'

And Turban charged Sikhs

The first time I visited Scotland's capital was in the late 1970s. A friend drove my family and me up to Edinburgh from Newcastle. On the way we stopped off in the Cheviot Hills to look in vain for some cloudberries—but we did find the berryless plants. I remember visiting the impressive Scottish National Art Gallery and the world famous Edinburg Castle. The second time was in October 2001 for the Scotland versus Ireland rugby. The match was postponed from March because of an outbreak of foot and mouth disease. Ireland had already beaten France and England so a grand slam chance was a possibility. Scotland was bottom of the table but alas, Ireland lost which is why six nations rugby can be so unpredictable. My son Ragnar and an old friend Andy were with me and we stayed with Andy's mother–in–law in Fife. We managed to walk the old golf course at St Andrews and one day I might get the chance to play a round of golf there.

On this marathon visit, I was on my own and booked into a small hotel in the New Town. It was the 12th June and light rain and a cold breeze greeted me when I stepped out onto Princess Street in the hearth of Edinburgh. My second day as a 59 year old was clearly going to be a bit of a challenge.

To get to the marathon start I had a mile walk down hill through the Old Town. The start was close to the new very costly parliament building at the back of Hollyrood Palace and in front of Arthur's Seat. It was just a 20 min warm-up walk for a 9.00 am start. The course was one lap which, as well as the city centre, included a wonderful coastal 10km stretch along the Firth of Forth and a hilly final 8km back to the city.

The first four miles were back into and around the city. A bit odd to do all the scenic bit at the start when many people are still in bed. Still it was good to be running with 7000 people plus 4000 relay runners. The early pace was 8 minutes a mile or 5 minutes per kilometre – too fast really. I found the hilly streets ok—even the ones with their cobbled stones. After the trip through the old and new towns, we arrived back at the new parliament and again ran right through the start—an unusual occurrence in marathons – and on out into open country towards the Firth of Forth.

I got talking to a runner wearing a green Hibernian football top whose wife was seriously ill in hospital. He felt guilty about running and not being with her but she was clearly in his thoughts. I was able to glean enough information from him to be able to send her a get-well card and let her know how much she was in her husband's thoughts. Later I managed to visit the Hibernian football club at Easter Road not far from the old city. Hibernian and Hearts, the other premiership club in the city, have a similar but less intense rivalry than Celtic and Rangers in Glasgow. Like Celtic, Hibernian was founded by a catholic priest for the immigrant Irish and is older than its Glasgow counterpart.

On the long coastal run, I had a conversation with a runner from South Africa who was running his fifth marathon on his fifth continent. I concluded that he must be rich and asked him if he supported any charities. He gave me a clear 'NO' for an answer and added that he did not believe in charity. I am thankful that he is very much in the minority when it comes to runners supporting charitable organisations.

A bit of colour was added to the marathon by the presence of a team of five running Sikhs whose combined age was 397 years. They were running as a relay team turban clad but not necessarily turbo charged—not to be expected at their age.

I struggled with the hills over the last 8 km. and had to resort to walking a little now and then up the steeper hills to get home in 3hr 56min.

I met a couple of Scottish men at my hotel prior to the marathon and we had a nice few celebratory drinks in the evening after the marathon. On of them came up by train from London and was a strict vegetarian. This did not stop him completing the run in less than 3hr 25min. His friend did not compete. In fact he was an old unemployed school colleague from north of Glasgow who collected the local club programmes for his London based friend who gave him some financial support. In this case charity dose begin 'at home'.

As I write, I still have to run in Wales to complete the British part of my marathon journey. The job of marathon running is never finished.

THREE COUNTRIES IN ONE MARATHON

36M MARATHON DE MONACO 17TH NOV 2002

Running in three countries—Monaco-France –Italy

Does Monaco qualify as a separate country in my list of marathon countries? Well it certainly is an independent country if we use the criteria of the number of tax exiles living there and the plethora of domicile regulations. As well as a tax haven for the super rich it can claim an established royal family and the world famous Monaco Grand Prix. It was a country judged well enough for the Irish-American actor Grace Kelly to find and marry her Prince Charming. Consequently, I judged that that it was good enough to qualify as one of my marathon countries. In fact, I got three countries for the price of one as the marathon course included parts of Italy and France.

It was too expensive—and a little constricted for me—to stay in Monte Carlo, so I based myself in nearby Nice on the French Riviera with its famous Promenade Anglaise. My stay in Nice was blessed by fine sunny weather in contrast to the dull, dark, damp and grey mid-November weather that I left behind in England. I could now understand why the well-to-do English flocked to the Riviera in the winter months. During the week prior to the marathon, I had a heavy head cold, but luckily it did not go down into my chest and it dried up on the Friday before my Saturday departure. This allowed me to get a good invigorating swim in on Friday morning after a week of non running. Previously I got in a 65min, 70min and 90min runs, which again left me short of a long stamina run to help with the last six kilometres of the marathon—but I have been here before in terms of marathon preparation.

After arrival on Saturday and checking in at my small hotel, I made my way to Monte Carlo by train. It came as a surprise that Monte Carlo's train station is inside a mountain with an 800-meter walk to the exit. The city is built into the side of a small mountain overlooking expensive yacht harbours and includes large blocks of flats interwoven between roads with plenty of hairpin bends. All runners had to register at the city's only football stadium built over an underground car park.

On the Sunday morning of the marathon, I was up at 6.45am, had a good breakfast and got the 7.35am train to Monte Carlo. I was lucky to get a bus to the stadium to drop off spare clothing but then had to get another bus to the start, which was nearly 2km away.

Whilst limbering up in the start area I had a chat with a couple from Minnesota who recommended that I run their lakeside marathon in their home state. In 2009 – seven years later – I met two teachers from Minnesota in Ireland whilst walking the Dingle Way in Kerry who also recommended that I run the Lakeside marathon. They offered to play host to me. I tried to enter the race when I got back to England but it was full – almost four months before the starting date.

I still at the time of writing this not got to Minnesota.

As it was such a lovely day I decided to run in running vest but with leggings over my running shorts. The first 5km was surprisingly easy mainly because it was on hairpin bends going down towards the shoreline; but the next 5km were a continuous climb up to give a fantastic view of the coastline towards Italy. The good news was that I would be returning the same way when it would be down hill. From 14km, there was a long downhill to the Baie des Anges and then an uphill motorway (closed to traffic) through two tunnels into Italy. Another easy downhill took me to the first town in Italy. At 31km, I had to face a stiff climb back up into Monaco. I passed two English runners and boasted that the hill was no problem. One kilometre later on one of them passed me saying the hill was no problem! Still I tried to give myself a boost, which nearly got me all the way up the hill, but near the top I had to walk. The lovely sunlit coastline came into view and the high-rise flats of Monte Carlo were now clearly visible. A sustained effort got me home in 3hr 52 Min, which was pleasing enough. I had a little shock at the end by having to run up quite a rocky steep climb to get into the main stadium entrance. I could have done with one of those cars in the car park beneath the stadium. Body wise I only suffered a painful left foot and Achilles tendon but no calf muscle problems. I met one other Irishman before the race who was hoping for a time of 3.30 but had a disappointing 3.55. He told me that he was a recovering alcoholic so the marathon was now his tonic of choice. I spent the evening celebrating with him and he drank a cup of coffee to my every beer.

On my way back to the station I popped into a shop to buy some postcards and got talking to the woman owner. She was impressed with my marathon run and even more impressed with the fact that someone from Ireland came to run it. Not alone did she give me several free postcards but also some T-Shirts depicting the Monte Carlo Grand Prix. I took the train back to Nice feeling a little extra glow of happiness. Yes, you do meet some generous people on one's travels.

RUNNING FOR THE GIRLS AND MOZART

42M THE MOZART VIENNA CITY MARATHON MAY 2006

Celebrating Mozart's 250th Birthday.

For nearly 30 years Austria along with Norway have been the venues for our annual skiing experiences. In Austria we have always gone to the St Johann – Kitzbuhl area and I have even had a ski run on the famous Hamennkahn downhill. At first, we went with parties of schoolchildren, but lately we have organised our own adult party using the same hotel and facilities that we used with the school parties. I have done many training runs on snow clad mountain paths at San Johann for spring marathons but cannot really explain why I took so long to run one in Austria. Austria was to be my 25th country to run in.

I was teaching at St Paul's School for Girls in London, which is recognised as one of the most elite schools in the UK with some 60% of the girls winning places at Oxbridge. Each year the girls at St Pauls vote for two charities to support – one local and one international. In 2006, they voted to support the local St Clements' and St James' parish after school club and The African Micro-Loan Scheme supporting business set up schemes on that continent.

My daughter Astrid, a student vacation ski-instructor at St Johann was also coming with me, in her case to run the half-marathon and to meet up again with some Austrian friends.

As part of my sponsorship raising activities, I intended to give a school assembly at St Pauls and with such bright and freethinking girls; it had to be a good one, especially as I wanted some of their money. To catch their interest I decided to reveal the country and venue for my marathon by live internet-connection at the end of the assembly. I was very fortunate that the marathon that I selected had a musical connection which I knew would appeal to the girls, most of whom played a classical instrument, and after all the international composer Gustav Holst – he of the Planet Suite – was Head of Music at the school for many years and composed most of his music there. I will describe my school assemblies on marathon running elsewhere, but suffice it to state here that the marathon selected was The Mozart Vienna City Marathon in honour of his 250th birthday.

My training for this marathon was average by my standards, especially in view of my daily commute from Hertford to Hammersmith in London, which involved a 10 minute bike ride to Hertford station, 40 minute train journey, 35 minute tube journey and 15 minute walk to the school. Despite a heavy timetable and the 'challenging demands and needs' of the young ladies in my charge, I managed to squeeze in some 35 minute lunchtime runs. I discovered a nice course that took me out over Hammersmith Bridge and along a very pleasant Thames footpath to Putney Bridge and back to the school via Fulham Football Club. I did manage to have a quick shower – not too many male showers in a girl's school – a sandwich and then straight to lessons. Unfortunately, I need at least a half hour to cool down after a run so I do not know what the girls thought about their sweaty teacher in their lesson.

Our trip to Vienna was my now familiar out Friday evening back Sunday evening effort, which allowed for a little socializing and a few drinks on the Friday night. Saturday was registration as usual with a little bit of sight seeing and a nice Italian meal with my daughter and her Viennese friends in the evening.

The race started right next to The United Nations Centre and then crossed the magnificent Danube River into old Vienna. It was a single lap course taking in all the main sights of the city. The race attracted well over 10,000 runners for the marathon and half-marathon and was a bit crowded for the first 10km, which resulted in my daughter and I running a little too slow. This was especially the case for my daughter who wanted a half-marathon time less than 1hr 45 min. She did push ahead through the field to finish in 1hr

52min but still had plenty of energy left. Crowded city marathons are not always the best places to achieve a PB as I have learnt to my cost on many occasions. As for me, my time for the half-marathon of 1hr 58min was slower than my average for this part of the race, and normally I run the second half up to 10 minutes slower than the first half. However, on this occasion I managed to run the second half in a similar time to the first and finished in 3hr 56min.

As we ran round the course, we were treated to the music of Mozart coming from loudspeakers along the course. It was not until going in a large park that I thought the music sounded live and was not taped. Sure enough as I rounded a corner, I saw to my left the full Vienna Philharmonic Orchestra playing at full throttle dressed in all their finery. It was a truly uplifting experience and put an extra bounce into my running all the way to the finishing line. Our marathon medals depicted Mozart and included some musical notes from one of his symphonies, a very welcome and unique addition to my medal collection.

Afterwards my daughter and I enjoyed a relaxed drink on a sunny terrace and then enjoyed some real Viennese cuisine in a local restaurant before heading back to London. My time and marathon place position were emailed to St Pauls so that the girls and staff could see the result on the school's information monitors as they came into school on Monday morning. This was part of the build up to doing the hard bit – collecting in the sponsorship money, which I am pleased to state, was well over £1000.

1ST COLOGNE MARATHON SEPT 1997

24M SEPT 1997

FINISHING COLOGNE MARATHON 1997

My primary reason for running in this marathon was to visit German friends who lived in the towns of Bruhl and Bonn and my wife was happy to join me. Surprisingly it was the first marathon to take place in Cologne and was well sponsored by the Ford Motor Company who had a large car factory in the city.

Cologne was founded by the Romans and is located on the west bank of the Rhine. It was heavily bombed during the Second World War but its famous Cathedral (The Dom) survived. The cathedral was finally completed in the late 19th century after some 700 years of construction. For many years on our school trips to Germany, I took the opportunity to race the pupils up the 400 + steps of the spiral staircase into one of the twin spires. I cheated a bit by making sure I got an early start—it is difficult to pass someone ahead of you on a spiral staircase. The city is also famous for its Carnival celebrations in February and of course its beer. Their local beer is Kolsh and is top fermented like English Real Ale. The locals like to drink the Kolsh in small 250cl straight glasses. You just have to drink more of them.

The start of the marathon was on the east side of the Rhine and the views as we crossed the main bridge over the river were very inspiring. After several kilometres going to the north and then to the south of the city along the Rhine, we finished right in front of the Cathedral.

This marathon was unusual as far as they had a roller skate marathon for the start. I believe the winner finished well under 90 minutes.

As for me, I had a very good race, in very favourable weather conditions and finished in 3hours 32 minutes and that was a very good run for a then 51 year old.

Afterwards we went to the Old Town for a Kolsh of Course.

MUNICH MARATHON

47M OCTOBER 2007

My daughter studied at Munich University for a year in 2007-8 as part of her law degree at University College London. In September 2007 I dro ve her with a lot of luggage to Munich and helped her settle in to her new flat and returned again in October to run the marathon with her and her friends support.

Munich centre is relatively small as cities go but it does have the famous Hofbrauhaus and October Beer festival. It is also the home of BMW the German car manufacturer. The 1992 Olympics were held in the city and sadly is now best remembered for the terrorist attack on the Israeli athletes. The marathon started and finished in the Olympic Stadium.

My daughter, friends and I visited the Olympic Stadium the day before the marathon. There are some lovely walks in and around the Olympic Park. I was surprised and delighted to find that one of the walkways in the park was named after Gillian Board, a British athlete who got a silver medal in the 400 meters at the Mexico City Olympics in 1968. She also won gold medals in the European Championships. Sadly, Lillian contracted bowel cancer and died in a Munich hospital at the age of only 22 years.

The one memorable part of the course was running several kilometres through the English Garden which was designed by an American loyalist Lord and others in the later part of the 18th century.The last 10 km was mostly around the city centre with splendid views of the Fraue Kirche.

The weather was sunny and cool, perfect conditions for a good run. My daughter and friends gave me some badly needed support at the 35km mark—in fact my daughter ran a kilometre with me. I had a big surprise at the 40km mark when two buxom blondes offered me and other runners large steins of Munich beer; but the thought of drinking gassy beer at this stage of the marathon was just too much for me. More beer was offered in the stadium after the finish but alas I need a few hours recovery before partaking of the amber nectar! I was pleased with my time 3hr 55min. We celebrated with a nice meal in the evening and the next day I said goodbye to my daughter Astrid and headed back to London.

MILAN MARATHON—THE ICE MAN COMETH

54M APRIL 2011

NEAR THE FINISH IN FRONT OF THE DOM MILAN MARATHON 2010 30C TEMP

April 2011 was one of the hottest months in Europe for many years. Easter was late that year so our annual ski trip to Norway would not be until the latter part of April. I took the opportunity to get a marathon in before then.

I was having problems with my neck for a couple of months. My son Fingal had given me some exercises to do which helped a bit. Still I had to run this marathon unable to move my head easily from side to side. As a result, I did not engage in conversation with the other runners. I also had to cope with the heat and my mysterious lack of stamina. Little did I know that eleven months later I would have a double heart bypass.

My wife and I have always liked the South Tyrol and the fact that in this part of Italy the inhabitants are German speakers. This marathon was going to be a bit of a holiday. We hired a car and spent a week in Bergamo and Bolzano (Bozen in German) before going to Milan for the marathon.

One of the highlights of the trip was a visit to the new museum dedicated to The Glacier Mummy. Around 5,300 years ago, a man was travelling through the Otz Valley in the Alps with damaged equipment and without food. High up in the icy mountains he met his death. Thousands of years later he was excavated from the ice as a deep-dry-frozen mummy and became know all over the world by the nickname 'Otzi' after the valley where he was found. The melting glacier revealed a body so well preserved that one could observe tattoos on the man's heels and back as well his bearskin hat, shoes, coat and medicine bag etc.

Otzi's body was discovered at 3200 metres above sea level and he probably bled to death from an arrow head lodged in his left shoulder as he tried to escape. His last journey covered tens of kilometres at rising altitude and in freezing conditions – a true marathon effort that ended in death. His high fitness level could have come from years of droving sheep and goats to graze in high mountain pastures. Was Otzi one of the first humans to discover fitness through high altitude training?

Milan is an old city with a fine Cathedral and famous shopping and fashion centre. It has wide streets lined by large apartment blocks. When it comes to Italian cities, I prefer Rome, Florence and Venice. The day before the marathon, my wife and I paid a small fortune for a coffee and orange juices near the centre. I had to have some carbohydrates and needed to order two pizzas at an exorbitant price and this did not endear me to this city.

The start of the marathon was at a very uninspiring business complex some thirty kilometres from the finish in the centre of the city. The first few kilometres were in pleasant countryside at a very comfortable temperature. My neck problems prevented me from trying to engage with other runners. Soon we approached the city outskirts as the heat began to build up. We ran past the famous San Siro football stadium, which looked like a large spaceship on four giant spiral (actually external staircases) springs. The stadium was surrounded by desolate lunar landscape like car parks. I am reliable informed that the stadium is very attractive inside.

My main memory of running in the city centre is of long wide streets with large cobbled stoned intersections lined with tram tracks. The temperature reached 30 C and the last couple of kilometres around the cathedral and towards the finish were the most atmospheric section of the marathon. My time of 4 hours 22 minutes was my slowest ever but at least I finished.

My wife and I had a tube ride and a long walk back to our hotel. Keeping warm was not a problem in the heat. That evening we had a satisfactory meal and a good but expensive bottle of wine. At the table next to us we talked to a Swedish mother and daughter who had ordered the house wine which they though did not taste good. I tasted it and thought of weak sweet carbonated water. They then selected the same wine as we had. Do not order Italian house wine is the message here.

MALTA LAND ROVER 25TH MARATHON

52M FEBRUARY 2010—THE WRONG WAY HOME

For such a small island set between North Africa and Southern Italy, Malta has an extraordinary history. St Paul visited this island before his execution in Rome. The Crusaders finally settled on the island after the last Crusades and became known as The Knights of Malta. It was the island that stood up to years of bombardment by the German Luftwaffe during World War 2 and as recognition of their war effort; the whole island was awarded The George Cross.

History aside, Malta has some great rabbit dishes and produces a liqueur from the local Prickly Pears. Its buses are old English Bedfords from the 1950s with self-employed drivers and going on one is akin to a roller-coaster ride. (Update: the latest London rejected bendy buses sadly have now replaced these). It is also good value for money. I stayed in the 4Star Cavalieri Hotel just north of the capital Valletta for five days with taxi pickup and drop off at the airport for less than £180. The island had no rain for several months and there was a dusting of red sand blown over from the Sahara on many car tops and shop windows. This sand in the atmosphere can give the locals an unpleasant dry throat and chesty cough. I was fortunate that the marathon was at the start of my stay in Malta so I was unaffected.

The marathon start was inland in the old hilltop former capital Mdina. At the start, I met two English girls who had run with me in the Riga, Latvia marathon – small world. It was a beautiful clear cool sunny morning and the first 5km downhill run gave time to admire the distant view of Valletta and the blue Mediterranean sea beyond. Things got tougher when we had to cope with a long uphill climb to the national stadium in the centre of the island. It was here and to my astonishment, I saw two of the lead runners coming towards us. Only later did I find out that they were disqualified from the race. The lead car had managed to get too far ahead of them and lose them in the roads around the stadium. It was a big embarrassment for the race organisers and the sponsors Land Rover.

The last 20km were through undulating countryside past many prickly pear plants—a liqueur and soda mix would have been nice at this stage—to finish in Vallette. My time of 4-hours 12 minutes was a little disappointing but I was not able to get in enough training over the Christmas period and during January.

During the next few days I was able to go roller-coasting again on Malta's buses. I visited a World War 2 museum, St John' Cathedral and went back to see around the old capital Mdina with its magnificent St Paul's Cathedral. At the Cathedral in Valletta, I saw a wonderful painting by Caravaggio – The Beheading of St John the Baptist. At least our two disqualified runners did not suffer that fate!

I enjoyed my stay on the island so much that my wife and I returned in November of the following year for a week's winter holiday.

NICE TO CANNES—A RUN ALONG THE FRENCH RIVIERA

51M 8TH NOV 2009

For this marathon I was joined by my sister Avril from Canada and two Belgian friends. The area was familiar to me as I had stayed in Nice when I ran the Monaco marathon. This time the marathon would start in Nice and go down along the coast through Cagnes sur Mer and around the Antibes peninsula to Cannes.

We were able to spend a few days sightseeing using Nice's impressive tram system. My sister and I visited Monaco for the day and resisted the temptation to spend time in the Casino. We also took a train up into the Alps towards the Italian border and back through Ventimiglia in Italy and back to Nice. In a pretty village near the border in freezing temperatures—compared to 16c in Nice – I was surprised by the amount of dog pooh all over the place. My sister loves dogs and as she was away from her beloved Guinness back in Toronto, she needed to pick up every small dog for a quick cuddle. This endeared her to various French woman dog owners, some of who carried their dogs in large handbags and seated them in pride of place on their laps in restaurants as well. If only they would learn to scoop up their dog's mess!

The weather on race day was perfect for running—cool, sunny and no wind. The race started on the famous Promenade de Anglais. There was plenty to see as we ran through several coastal towns to Cannes. There was just one hilly section around Antibes but here I had the support of my three fans. At the finish I could not find my sister et al so took the train back to our hotel in Nice and to a nice hot bath—always a top priority of mine. Again, I just managed to break the 4-hour barrier with a time of 3hours 58 min.

BENEDORM – A RUN ALONG THE SEAFRONT

53M NOVEMBER 2010

Since I retired a few years ago I like to get a little bit of sunshine and my vitamin C fix before or after Christmas and if I can get a good run in so much the better. The temperature in Benidorm in mid-November is around 20C max and ideal for a marathon. My wife and I had two sets of friends to see in the area: a Belgian couple who were over wintering there and our eldest son Ragnar's parents-in-law. We used the services of a Sports Tour company and stayed for a week in a good hotel in central Benidorm only a few hundred meters from the start and finish of the marathon. The half-marathon was held the night before the marathon in torrential rain; but for the marathon itself it was beautiful and sunny with little wind and a great chance for me to top up my vitamin C level.

A few days before the marathon, my wife and I had a training session with our son's parents—in-laws and 6 bottles of red and two bottles of white wine were consumed. We held a similar training session with our Belgian friends; but this time the main fuel was Belgian beer. The day before the marathon was a day of strict abstinence and sleep.

The marathon course was two laps with two long climbs away from the beach area and two very enjoyable and scenic runs along both of Benidorm's beaches. Benidorm in winter is very different and far more pleasant from the crowded and disco nightclubs of Benidorm in the summer months. I was pleased with my time of 4 hours 9 min. But would have liked to break the 4-hour mark. I was 64 years old at the time so I think it was quite a respectable effort. I felt that I struggled more than usual in the early stages of the race and I struggled with my training runs in Austria the previous February at high altitude. Little did I know that these signs were not down to old age but a growing coronary heart blockage. Sixteen months on from Benidorm, I would need a heart double bypass for a 99% blockage of two of the heart's three main coronaries!

A couple of days after the marathon our friends drove us to the hilltop village of Guadalest. One notable memory is a visit to the local cemetery where one could not help but notice that most of the villagers buried there lived to eighty years or more. My conclusion was that living at altitude and a lifetime of walking up and down steep streets must be good for you.

EPILOGUE – THE ROAD AHEAD

It has taken some time to recover from my heart bypass in March 2012. I got back to walking and easy swimming after two months. By August—and during The London Olympics—I ran 12 km at about 6km pace and was feeling good. However, I had a set back at the end of August when my hearth went into atrial flutter so I had to take it easy. In October, shock treatment stabilised my heartbeat and I was able to start jogging again.

In April 2013, I ran my first competitive race – 10km in Hertford—in a time of 60 minutes. In October, I ran the toughest cross-country ultra half-marathon that I have ever participated in. My time of 2hours 24 minutes was my slowest ever—my best in 1983 was 1hour 24 minutes. Then I was much younger and did not have 15 hills, muck and high winds to cope with.

As for the future, I would like to run a few more easy marathons, starting maybe with London or Paris in 2014 in support of the heart research charity CORDA, but just to keep on running as long as I can will be my main aim.

Happy running and May the road rise up to meet you and the Sun be always on your back.

SEAN O'REILLY

MARATHON TIMES 1984-2013

1. 1984 LONDON 3HR 09MIN ENGLAND

2 1984 HARLOW 3HR 15MIN

3. 1988 LONDON 3HR 27MIN

4. 1988 PARIS 3HR 25MIN FRANCE

5. 1988 DUBLIN 3HR 28MIN IRELAND

6. 1989 LONDON 3HR 25MIN

7. 1989 ATHENS 3HR 27MIN GREECE

8. 1990 BERLIN 3HR 28MIN GERMANY

9. 1991 ROTTERDAM 3HR 23MIN HOLLAND

10.1992 LONDON 3HR 23MIN

11.1992 BRUSSELS 3HR 27MIN BELGIUM

12.1993 BOSTON 97TH 3HR 43MIN USA

13.1993 ANTWERP 3HR 21MIN

14.1993 ST ALBANS 3HR 35MIN

15.1994 LONDON 3HR 34MIN

16.1994 CHERBOURGE 3HR 30MIN

17.1994 ABINGDON 3HR 29MIN

18.1994 NEW YORK 3HR 39MIN

19.1995 HELSINKI 3HR 36MIN FINLAND

20.1995 REIMS 3HR 32MIN

21.1996 BOSTON 100TH 3HR 52MIN

22.1996 STOCKHOLM 3HR 43MIN SWEDEN

23.1997 ANTWERP 3HR 36MN

24.1997 COLOGNE 1ST 3HR 31MIN

25.1997 DUBLIN 3HR 42MIN

26.1998 LONDON 3HR 45MIN

27.1998 OSLO 3HR 42MIN NORWAY

28.1999 ROME 3HR 47MIN ITALY

29.1999 TORONTO 3HR 32MIN CANADA

30.2000 BARCELONA 3HR 36MIN SPAIN

31.2000 COPENHAGEN 4HR 05MIN DENMARK

32.2000 LISBON 4HR 06MIN Portugal

33.2001 PRAGUE 3HR 37MIN CZECK REPUBLIC

34.2001 NIAGARA FALLS 4HR 05MIN

35.2002 BUDAPEST 3HR 46MIN HUNGARY

36.2002 MONACO 3HR 52MIN MONACA

37 2003 IS TANBUL 3HR 58MIN TURKEY

38 2003 REYKJAVIK 3HR 54MIN ICELAND

39 2004 OOSTENDE 3HR 48MIN

XX2004 CYPRUS 1HR 45MIN CYPRUS (HALF MARATHON-MARATHON CANCELLED)

40 2005 SANTIAGO 3HR 51MIN CHILE

41 2005 EDINBURG 3HR 56MIN SCOTLAND

42 2006 VIENNA 3HR 57 MIN AUSTRIA

43 2006 POZNAN 3HR 55 MIN POLAND

44 2006 BONN (Off Road) 4HR 13 MIN

45 2007 CORNWALL 3HR 59 MIN

46 2007 LEIDEN 4 HR 10 MIN

47 2007 MUNICH 3 HR 55 MIN

XX2008TALINN 45MIN ESTONIA (10KM MARATHON CANCELLED)

48 2008 ZURICH 4 HR 02 MIN SWITZERLAND

49 2008 LJUBLANSKI 3 HR 52 MIN SLOVENIA

50 2009 RIGA 3 HR 58 MIN LATVIA

51 2009 NICE-CANNES 3 HR 58 MIN

52 2010 MALTA 4 HR 12 MIN MALTA

53 2010 BENEDORM 4 HR 09 MIN

54 2011 MILAN 4 HR 13 MIN

AVERAGE TIME 41 MARATHONS = 3HR 36MIN

(OVER 21 YEARS)

11 marathons run since age 60 in 2006. Of these, 7 were under 4 hours and 4 over 4 hours.

Average Time 4 hours 1 min.

HOTTEST—HELSINKI 27'C

COLDEST—ROTTERDAM 5'C

WETTEST—NIAGARA FALLS!

Lightning Source UK Ltd.
Milton Keynes UK
UKOW06f0433120214

226298UK00010B/44/P

9 781491 886694